PORCH
PARTIES

PORCH PARTIES

COCKTAIL RECIPES *and* EASY IDEAS
FOR OUTDOOR ENTERTAINING

by Denise Gee

Photographs by Robert M. Peacock

CHRONICLE BOOKS

SAN FRANCISCO

CHEERS TO...

≫≫—→ Amy Treadwell at Chronicle Books, for conceptualizing this book and seeing that we were the right team to work on it. ≫≫—→ Sarah Billingsley, our editor at Chronicle—who's not only a skillful editor, but also a delightful person. And to the book's designer, Hallie Overman, for cleverly capturing the fun spirit of the project. ≫≫—→ Literary agent Angela Miller, for tooting our horn. ≫≫—→ Dempse McMullen for lending us some great collectibles for our photo shoots. ≫≫—→ Edith Peacock, for assisting us both on shoots and afterward; and George and Joyce Peacock for cheering us on in a big Texas way. ≫≫—→ Eddie Maestri (plus Adam Moore, Nan Moore, Nelda Brooks, and Parker), for the use of his Dallas porches and helping make them fabulous for photography. ≫≫—→ Darby and Dennis Short, of downtown Natchez, Mississippi, for use of their dreamy front gallery and back porch. ≫≫—→ Linda and Tom Scarritt, whose wraparound porch in Tampa, Florida, is as cool, colorful, and gracious as they come. ≫≫—→ Kirk Kirksey, whose Winnetka Heights porch became one of our makeshift studios. ≫≫—→ Julie Martin and Michael Sunich of Tampa: Thanks for letting us capture a bit of Old Florida at your Full Circle Farm in Dover. ≫≫—→ Jenny O'Connor for helping with research. ≫≫—→ Alfie the standard poodle for "assisting" during our shoots in his own special way. ≫≫—→ All our family and friends who we hope to be seeing on our porch—and their porches—very soon.

Library of Congress Cataloging-in-Publication Data available.

ISBN 978-0-8118-6580-7

Manufactured in China.

Designed by Hallie Overman, Brooklyn, New York.
Food and prop styling by Denise Gee.

10 9 8 7 6 5 4

Chronicle Books LLC
680 Second Street
San Francisco, California 94107
www.chroniclebooks.com

DEDICATED
TO

The good people of
Historic Winnetka Heights in Dallas,
Hyde Park in Tampa,
and all other porch-centric communities
for preserving the joy of architecture and
neighborly camaraderie.

table of contents

CHAPTER
No.3
PUNCH WITH PIZZAZZ

CHAPTER
No.4
THINK FROCKTAILS NOT MOCKTAILS

CHAPTER
No.5
LITTLE BITES

INTRODUCTION

Come Sit for a Spell.

THERE'S SOMETHING INSTANTLY RELAXING ABOUT A PORCH,
WHERE—IN YOUR OWN HOME, A FRIEND'S HOME, OR A FAVORITE RENTAL
COTTAGE—YOU CAN RELAX IN YOUR OWN LITTLE WORLD.

Perhaps that's just having your feet propped up while you sway in a swing. Or being able to lean back in an Adirondack chair, drink in hand, while savoring both the beverage and the aroma of dinner wafting out from the kitchen. In these hurried days, such scenarios are priceless.

The true height of enjoyment, though, is to share that experience with friends and family. On such occasions, festive drinks (Pomegranate Pimm's Cup, anyone?) and uncomplicated but interesting food (care for some Greek Crostini?) are a must. And that's what this book is about—giving you the tools you need to extend such an invitation and fulfill it effortlessly and brilliantly.

Beyond that, this book is also about setting a party stage with the right decor and ambiance. Nowadays there are plenty more options than just porch swings, basic wood fans, and rockers. How about swinging porch beds, fireplaces, outdoor rugs, and living room furniture? With all of that, one could practically live outside. I really could. Actually, I have.

While I was growing up near Natchez, Mississippi, our family owned property on nearby Lake Concordia that had a unique structure: a giant enclosed screened building that we called "the Porch." Technically it wasn't a porch because it was freestanding, but its purpose was all porch. Though it no longer stands (it was torn down to build a house atop the site), I can close my eyes and am instantly transported there.

I hear the screen door's rusty springs as I head inside. There's the oversize fireplace, bar, and full-size refrigerator-freezer; the strings of party lights and the slow-moving, moaning ceiling fans; the musty chaise lounges where we'd read or nap, the big center table where we'd eat and play cards, and the smaller tables along the screened walls that hosted other pastimes (card tricks or checkers, maybe). I hear the stereo where music (the iconic song "Rock the Boat" by the Hues Corporation is playing) could reach our pier and boathouse. I see the warped Irish drinking proverb signs my grandmother and grandfather collected over the years. And the long buffet table, where a boatload of food (smoked brisket and fried fish, chiefly) will soon be spread out for all those we've invited for an afternoon-evening-overnight gathering. With that, I don't want to ever open my eyes. I don't want to leave. I so miss that place. Maybe that's why, in the homes I've lived in, having a porch has been a must, and keeping in tune with hospitable surroundings has particularly interested me.

Over the years that I've worked as both a food and home design editor, I've discovered that many people feel the same as I do. And I'm delighted to learn that in the United States we are building more porches. According to the National Association of Home Builders, nearly 60 percent of new, single-family homes were built with porches as of 2007 (up from 39 percent in 1996). That says a lot about the importance of outdoor living in our lives.

I've also learned that the porch mindset travels with us wherever we are—be it in a condo (where even a small deck is a getaway), or a bed-and-breakfast (I'm sure the most successful ones have porches), or modern rooftops geared to entertaining. It's all about taking it outside and letting our cares blow away with the breeze. To savor a quick and rejuvenating respite. To talk with each other and share stories that might otherwise get lost in the doldrums of everyday life.

It's been said a porch is where a home welcomes you with open arms. With this book, I hope you truly feel the warm welcome.

LISTEN TO THE GENTLE CREAK OF A ROCKING CHAIR

ON AN OLD WOODEN PORCH, OR FEEL YOUR FIRST UPLIFTING BREEZE ON A DECK: YOU KNOW YOU'RE IN THE RIGHT PLACE TO WASH YOUR CARES AWAY. THAT'S EVEN MORE TRUE IF YOU'RE HOLDING A REFRESHING BEVERAGE—*AND IT'S ESPECIALLY MEMORABLE WHEN SHARED* IN THE COMPANY OF GOOD FRIENDS.

PORCH PARTY POINTERS

➤➤➤➤➤➤➤➤➤➤➤➤➤➤➤➤➤→

COMFORT AND JOY
PORCH DECOR *and* AMBIANCE

WE'RE LUCKY THAT THERE'S SO MUCH ATTENTION BEING PAID TO OUTDOOR LIVING STYLE.

IT IS THE GREENEST WAY YOU CAN LIVE, RIGHT? CONSIDER THE LATEST TRENDS IN OUTDOOR FINERY AND FUNCTION.

LIGHTING

String party lights around the perimeter of your porch and line walkways leading to it with decorative paper bags weighted down with sand and small votives. If your porch is practically another living area for you, invest in an indoor-outdoor lamp or two (some are really smart looking) to avoid having that one glaring ceiling-fan light. Candles under hurricane glass enclosures are always nice, as are sconces in low-traveled areas, but always be sure to use candles only if you'll be around them while in use. Tiki torches visible from your porch are also great for the right setting. And if you can muster up some fireflies to pay a visit, you'll win the day.

MUSIC

Music is a must for any gathering other than a wake (which, on occasion, later in the evening, might even call for music, too). Enlist water-resistant built-in or outdoor speakers; they're not that expensive and are easy to set up. If you're not computer-savvy, have someone who is help you set up some playlists on your computer; playlists allow you to play music (downloaded Cajun or Zydeco music, if you're having, say, a Mardi Gras party) on a cycle mode throughout the evening, worry-free. Just remember to let the neighbors know in advance that you're having a party (and inviting them always helps) and do keep the music from blaring.

FLOORING

Dress it up a bit. There are numerous simple and decorative outdoor-rated rugs to help define spaces (and that are easy to hose down after the party). For a more dramatic look atop concrete, use snap-in-place teak or cypress squares in various patterns. Or, just have your concrete painted and polished. For wood, keep it freshly painted and even consider having it look swell with a wide checkerboard design in subtle contrasting colors (i.e., soft green and cream).

HEATING AND COOLING

Ceiling fans have never been more decorative than they are now, so your options are much better than they used to be. Just remember to look for ones rated indoor-outdoor. As for heating, if your ceilings are tall enough, and if you like to use your porch even when it's nippy, consider buying one or two standing heaters that cut the chill factor and warm up the place.

Fireplaces are also making appearances more and more on porches— some with technology that allows you to enjoy the same two-sided fireplace both indoors and out.

FURNITURE

Furnishings in weather-hearty cypress, teak, and some of the newer exotic woods—like the Brazilian wood ipé—will last for years and weather beautifully. As for the new resin wickers, well, those hard-woven options will fool anyone's eye. Moving ahead of materials are the new forms being enjoyed— outdoor furnishings in Louis XVI style? I love it. And the stark-white or vividly

colored pieces made of molded polypropylene? Ditto. Porch swings and rockers are de rigueur but now there are even swinging daybeds for enjoyment. As an aside, literally, do plan to have enough side table options at your parties—even if they're just folding tables with tablecloths. Having a place to set down a drink or plate is a wonderful thing.

FABRIC

All-weather fabric that's resistant to dirt buildup and mildew makes decorating *sooo* much nicer. Sunbrella brand has been a leader in this category, but options run the gamut, with both top designers and discount department stores getting in on the indoor-outdoor living revolution. They're offering not the plain-Jane fabrics of the past but instead, lots of bright colors and sophisticated patterns. I love that there are even outdoor curtains you can hang to soften a porch's "walls" and offer privacy.

HOORAY FOR THE BUFFET
PLANNING IDEAS

Porches lend themselves perfectly for hosting
LONG SERVING TABLES THAT CAN BE USED TO LET PEOPLE HELP THEMSELVES
(WHICH, IN TURN, HELPS YOU RELAX AND ENJOY THE PARTY MORE).
CONSIDER THESE TIPS ON MAKING THE MOST OF A BUFFET STATION.

GO WITH THE FLOW Place the buffet table in an area that, if possible, is close to the kitchen for replenishing food and also in a spot that won't cause people-traffic jams. Also, make sure the bar is separate from the buffet station or you'll really have a pileup.

MOOD LIFT To elevate your food for a more dramatic flair, set up cloth-covered risers using small crates, boxes, bricks, telephone books, or anything else that's sturdy. Keep easy-to-reach items—accessible with tongs—in back, and make sure dips and hot foods are down low (to keep the spinach dip out of the brownies, if you follow my drift). Cake stands and tiered serving plates also can help break up the flatlining of a presentation.

PIECE BE WITH YOU Have a serving piece to go with each dish. It's never good to see someone using the potato salad spoon to access a piece of cake.

TELL IT LIKE IT IS Use small frames with nicely written or printed dish names. Or use place cards to tell diners what they are dishing up.

HAPPY ENDING Have silverware and napkins at the end, so people don't have to fumble with them (and usually drop them) while getting food.

BE KIND Try to serve food that only requires fingers or a fork.

KEEP IT REAL Use cloth table coverings and utensils with heft to avoid having torn paper tablecloths and broken plastic utensils. Paper napkins and plates are certainly acceptable and handy, since there are some nicer quality versions available in fun patterns. Plastic cups are fine for kids, but avoid using them for cocktails, since they can change the flavor of the drink (making it taste, well, like plastic). Glasses really do make the best impression, and you can either rent them from party stores or buy them for very little money and store them in the basement or attic in between parties.

BE CONSISTENT Try to keep the same decor theme—all white, blue, and yellow, for example, or all baskets or wood—for a pulled-together look.

REMEMBER TO RECYCLE Denote separate bins for plastic cups and bottles so you don't have to pick through the garbage can later.

SINGIN' THE PORCH CEILING BLUES: BLUE PORCH CEILINGS—IN EVERY SHADE FROM BRIGHT TURQUOISE TO PALE ROBIN'S EGG—FOUND THEIR WAY FROM THE CARIBBEAN AND MEXICO AND INTO THE SOUTH. FOR MANY YEARS, THE SOUTH CERTAINLY HELD THE RECORD (IF THERE WAS ONE) FOR HAVING THE MOST BLUE PORCH CEILINGS IN THE COUNTRY; THAT WAS UNTIL RECENTLY, WHEN THE REST OF THE NATION BEGAN CATCHING ON TO THE SOOTHING LOOK. AS A CHILD IN THE SOUTH, I RECALL MY MOTHER NEVER THINKING OF IT AS AN AESTHETICS ISSUE BUT MORE AS A PRACTICAL ONE. "HAVING BLUE THERE TRICKS WASPS AND SPIDERS INTO THINKING IT'S THE SKY, SO THEY DON'T BUILD NESTS." THAT SEEMED PLAUSIBLE UNTIL I REALIZED HOW OFTEN I WAS SWEEPING THOSE NESTS AWAY BEFORE A PARTY. THAT SAID, MOST JUST PAINT THE CEILINGS BLUE TO CREATE A COOLING, CALMING EFFECT ON HOT DAYS. AND A SURPRISING NUMBER OF PEOPLE, MOSTLY ALONG THE GULF COAST, BELIEVE THAT BLUE SCARES AWAY EVIL SPIRITS. WHICH WOULD CERTAINLY BE AN ADDED BONUS IF TRUE.

GO FIGURE
PARTY PLANNING CHECKLIST

I'm a firm believer in the French term *mise en place*, or "everything in place." If you get what you need well in advance of your gathering, you can actually think about enjoying the party yourself.

SPIRITS

AFTER-DINNER LIQUEURS

BEER (VARIOUS LAGERS AND ALES)

BOURBON

BRANDY

GIN

ORANGE-FLAVORED LIQUEUR/TRIPLE SEC

RUM (LIGHT AND DARK)

SCOTCH

TEQUILA

VERMOUTH (DRY AND SWEET)

VODKA (PLAIN AND FLAVORED)

WHISKEY (TENNESSEE OR RYE)

WINES (PINOT GRIGIO, ROSÉ, AND PINOT NOIR ARE ALWAYS PLEASERS)

MIXERS

CLUB SODA

COLA (DIET AND REGULAR)

GINGER ALE

GRENADINE

ICE

ICED TEA, REFRIGERATED

JUICES (ORANGE, GRAPEFRUIT, CRANBERRY, TOMATO), FRESH, REFRIGERATED

LEMON-LIME FLAVORED SODA

LEMONADE OR LIMEADE, REFRIGERATED

NECTARS (PEACH, MANGO, PEAR)

SWEET-AND-SOUR MIX

TONIC WATER

WATER (BOTTLED SPARKLING OR STILL, OR PURIFIED TAP)

FLAVOR ENHANCERS

HORSERADISH

LEMONS, LIMES, ORANGES

MARASCHINO CHERRIES

OLD BAY OR SALT-FREE CREOLE SEASONING

OLIVES

PEPPER

RIMMING SALTS, FLAVORED

ROSE'S LIME JUICE

SEA SALT (KOSHER OR COARSE)

SIMPLE SYRUP (SEE SIMPLY DELICIOUS, PAGE 26)

SUPERFINE SUGAR

TABASCO SAUCE

WORCESTERSHIRE SAUCE

NECESSITIES

BAR SPOON, LONG-HANDLED

BAR TOWELS

BLENDER

BOTTLE OPENER

CAN OPENER

COCKTAIL PLATES

COCKTAIL SHAKER

COFFEE CUPS AND SAUCERS

COFFEEMAKER AND COFFEE (DECAF AND REGULAR); SUGAR AND CREAM

EATING UTENSILS, PLATES, GLASSES

FOLDING CHAIRS

FOLDING TABLES

ICE BUCKET, TONGS

ICE SCOOP

JIGGER

LUCITE CUTTING BOARD, SMALL

MEASURING CUP, SMALL

MIXING GLASS

MUDDLER

NAPKINS, COCKTAIL AND DINNER-SIZE

PARING KNIFE

PEELER/ZESTER

PITCHER

SERVING UTENSILS

STRAINER

TRASH CAN

WINE BOTTLE OPENER

OPTIONAL ACCESSORIES

ASHTRAYS

DRINK STIRRERS/PICKS/STRAWS

DRINKS TRAY

FESTIVE DRINK UMBRELLAS

NOVELTY ICE TRAYS

PLATES WITH BUILT-IN WINE GLASS HOLDERS

POUR SPOUTS

SPOONS, SMALL

STEMWARE CHARMS (FOR KEEPING TRACK OF GLASSES)

WOODEN SKEWERS, SMALL

DO TELL:

ONE BOTTLE OF WINE EQUALS 25.4 FLUID OUNCES, WHICH IS ABOUT FIVE SERVINGS PER BOTTLE. FIGURE ONE BOTTLE PER PERSON. A FIFTH OF LIQUOR PROVIDES ABOUT THIRTEEN 2-OUNCE POURS (FOR POTENT MARTINIS) AND ABOUT SIXTEEN 1-OUNCE SHOTS (FOR AVERAGE COCKTAILS). ONE LITER OF SODA EQUALS MORE THAN FIVE (6-OUNCE) SERVINGS. ONE BAG OF ICE WILL SERVE ABOUT SIX PEOPLE.

bar necessities
SETTING UP THE BAR

UNLESS YOUR PORCH SPORTS A BUILT-IN BAR/WET AREA (WHICH SOME OF THE NICEST ONES I'VE SEEN DO), THE REST OF US HAVE TO RELY ON OUR WITS. AND THESE IDEAS:

→ If using a galvanized aluminum basin to hold iced-down beer and wine and you don't have a stand for it, place it on a sturdy table topped with a vinyl tablecloth (I like using oilcloth with festive patterns). That makes any liquid cleanup a breeze.

→ At flea markets and antiques shops, be on the lookout for old porcelain baby bathtubs with their stands; they're not as cheap as they used to be, but they make marvelous places to stash ice, beer, sodas, and wine—and fun conversation pieces.

→ Some folks I know bought a great-looking vintage working refrigerator—in a cool shade of powder pink—just to keep on their porch. It's a fun look and a great way to keep both food and beverages chilled.

→ Ice chests are always convenient but not so attractive. My friend, *Better Homes and Gardens* designer Joe Boehm, once helped me transform a lidded lattice-box patio storage container into a clever concealer for an electric cooler (a good investment for parties that will last more than a couple of hours). The plug just threaded through the lattice, and off it went to the outlet box. We even painted it to match the setting's decor.

→ Multileveled planters, especially older ones, make perfect stations for bar items.

▶———▶ For a party with several dining tables, consider using leakproof ceramic planters on each table to keep wine chilled.

▶———▶ If freezer space is at a minimum, keep extra ice in a bathtub or washing machine, where the water will drain until you're ready to use the ice.

GLASS WITH CLASS
CONSIDER THE
DRINK AND THE GLASS

HAVING A COCKTAIL ON THE PORCH
ENCOURAGES SUCH A SENSE OF NOSTALGIA, I REACH FOR THE GLASSES MY
MOTHER AND GRANDMOTHER USED FOR THEIR "COCKTAIL HOUR."

I've also collected my own vintage glasses, especially enjoying many of them found via online auctions. I think this is becoming a trend with my friends, with all of us trying to outdo one another with the coolest vintage glasses we can find—giving new meaning to "you've been served."

ONLINE

CocktailShakers.com.....................fab collection of vintage shakers and retro barware
eBay.com.................................set up searches for favorite collectibles, dealers
PlaidPonyVintage.com...........................shop its housewares section for fun finds
RubyLane.com......................................it's just fun to dig around
Tias.com...ditto

LOCALLY

Antiques and collectibles shops
Church bazaars (*yes*, church-going
    folk do drink on occasion)
Estate and garage sales

WHEN BUYING OLD GLASSWARE, KEEP IN MIND

THAT 1930s MARTINI GLASSES ARE TINY IN COMPARISON TO TODAY'S
STEMWARE. I FOUND THAT OUT THE HARD WAY WHEN ORDERING A FABULOUS
SET THAT TURNED OUT IT COULD HAVE BEEN USED IN A DOLLHOUSE!

GLASS	GOOD FOR	HOLDS
CHAMPAGNE FLUTE	CHAMPAGNE/SPARKLING WINE	6 TO 8 OUNCES
COLLINS/HIGHBALL	FIZZY OR FRUITY DRINKS	10 TO 14 OUNCES
CORDIAL	AFTER-DINNER LIQUEURS	2 TO 4 OUNCES
HEAT-PROOF MUG	IRISH COFFEE (OR OTHER WARM BEVERAGE)	8 TO 10 OUNCES
MARGARITA	FROZEN OR ON-THE-ROCKS 'RITAS	12 OUNCES
MARTINI	STRONG, SLOW SIPPER DRINKS	4 TO 6 OUNCES
MUG/PINT	BEER	12 TO 16 OUNCES
OLD-FASHIONED OR ROCKS	COCKTAILS ON ICE	8 TO 10 OUNCES
PILSNER GLASS	BEER OR FIZZY DRINKS	12 TO 16 OUNCES
PUNCH CUP	ICY PUNCH	4 TO 6 OUNCES
SHOT GLASS	QUICK HITS OF LIQUOR	2 TO 3 OUNCES
SMALL OLD-FASHIONED	STRAIGHT-UP LIQUOR OR LOWBALL	4 TO 6 OUNCES
SNIFTER	BRANDY	5 TO 25 OUNCES
SOUR	OLD-FASHIONED COCKTAILS	6 OUNCES
RED WINE	FULL-BODIED RED WINE	10 TO 14 OUNCES
WHITE WINE	COOL WHITE WINE	6 TO 10 OUNCES

BE A GARNISH GOD(DESS)
FESTIVE DRINK EMBELLISHMENTS

CITRUS CURLS Use a vegetable peeler or small peel-slot on a quality zester to cut a citrus peel into a thin ¼-inch-wide spiral, rotating the utensil around the peel. After about two turns, taper off the spiral to complete the twist. Continue doing this with rest of peel. A stylist's trick is to curl the end around a straw or pencil and briefly freeze until needed.

CITRUS KNOTS Take long, thin curls or strips of citrus peel and carefully tie each into a knot.

CITRUS TWISTS Cut a lemon in half and slice ⅛ inch thick. Cut those slices in half diagonally before cutting the fruit and bitter pith away from each section of skin peel. Twist peel ends in opposite directions to release its oil into the drink. Either drop the peel into the drink or let it sit delicately on the lip of the glass. For long twists, dangle from the rim of the glass into the drink.

CITRUS WEDGES Using a sharp knife, cut off each end of the fruit. Cut in half lengthwise. With the rind side down, make one cut lengthwise down to, but not through, the rind. Turn over and slice into ¼- to ½-inch wedges.

CITRUS OR VEGETABLE WHEELS Cut a ¼-inch diagonal slice of a fruit or vegetable (such as a pineapple or cucumber) and make a long cut at one end, leaving the skin intact. Affix to the edge of the glass.

FESTIVE FRUIT Star fruit or carambola slices (gold indicates ripeness); kiwi slices (cut in half, gently scoop out of the fuzzy skin, and slice); partially sliced strawberries (hulls attached); peach or apple wedges; julienned apple "matchsticks" (with peel intact at the top).

FRUIT KABOBS Skewer a desired mix of grapes; berries; and orange, apple, pineapple sections; or whatever strikes your fancy.

VEGGIE STIRRERS Use green beans, celery stalks (leaves attached), vertical carrot slices, pickled okra.

OTHER SWEET IDEAS A whole vanilla bean, cinnamon stick, or peppermint stick; fresh coconut meat shavings, or chocolate shavings; candied ginger on skewers; frozen melon balls; sugarcane sticks/skewers; nutmeg sprinkles.

GOOD TIPS:

➡→ Slice lemons and limes the day before and keep them tightly wrapped in a plastic wrap covered dish or bowl or in a sealed container. Pull them out about an hour before the party.

➡→ Keep fruit skewers in a well sealed container; if you're concerned about fruit turning brown, keep them in a lemon-lime carbonated beverage.

SPRING SCREEN CLEANING AFTER WINTER'S HARSH WEATHER COMES SPRING, WHEN POLLEN FILLS THE AIR AND YOUR SCREENED-IN PORCH LOOKS BEATEN DOWN AND DINGY. FOR SCREEN CLEANING, USE A WINDOW-CLEANING ATTACHMENT FOR YOUR HOSE AND, WHILE HOSING THE SCREEN DOWN, GENTLY BRUSH OFF SOME OF THE MORE STUBBORN DIRT BUILDUP. ADDING A SMALL AMOUNT OF BLEACH TO THE CLEANING SOLUTION WILL ALSO KILL ANY MOLD THAT'S ACCUMULATED.

SIMPLY DELICIOUS
SIMPLE SYRUPS

SIMPLE SYRUPS ADD A WONDERFUL INFUSION OF FLAVOR.
THESE ARE MY FAVORITES—AND WILL BE YOURS, TOO, I BET.

SIMPLE SYRUP Combine 1 cup sugar and 1 cup water in a small saucepan. Heat to a boil while stirring. Reduce the heat and continue to stir until the sugar dissolves. Remove from heat and let cool. Pour the syrup into a clean container and store in the refrigerator indefinitely. Makes about 1½ cups.

GINGER SYRUP Combine 1 cup sugar and 1 cup water with ¼ cup peeled and chopped ginger in a medium saucepan. Heat to a boil while stirring. Reduce the heat and continue to stir until the sugar dissolves. Simmer, stirring occasionally, about 10 minutes or until the syrup has reduced by one-fourth. Remove from the heat and let cool. Pour the syrup through a small fine-mesh strainer fitted into a funnel into a clean container and store in the refrigerator for several months. Makes about 1¼ cups.

HONEY SYRUP Combine 1½ cups honey, ¼ cup water, ¼ cup fresh lemon juice, and ½ teaspoon grated lemon zest in a medium saucepan. Heat to a boil while stirring. Simmer, stirring occasionally, 10 minutes or until syrup has reduced by one-fourth. Remove from the heat and let cool. Pour the syrup into a clean container and store in the refrigerator for several months. Makes about 1¾ cups.

MINT SYRUP Combine 1 cup sugar and 1 cup water in a medium saucepan. Heat to a boil while stirring. Reduce the heat and continue to stir until the sugar dissolves. Add 12 to 14 fresh mint sprigs, set aside, and let cool. Pour the syrup through a fine-mesh strainer fitted into a funnel into a clean container and store in the refrigerator indefinitely. Makes about 1½ cups.

nice ice

NOVEL ICE IDEAS

DRESS UP YOUR COCKTAIL OR PUNCH BOWL WITH ICE
THAT'S JUST AS FESTIVE AS YOU ARE. TALK ABOUT FORM AND FUNCTIONALITY.

>>>——→ For the clearest ice—what I call "pristine" ice—boil some distilled (sans minerals) water in a very clean pot to avoid introducing any properties that might cloud the water. That'll make the water as pure as possible for freezing and hence, as clear as possible. Just know it won't be as pristinely clear as ice found in restaurants or commercial bags (they have special cooling processes that give ice an extra boost in the clarity category), but it'll be striking nonetheless.

>>>——→ For berries or herbs in ice, fill an ice tray two-thirds with distilled water and add to each slot an edible berry, or a mint or lemon verbena leaf; fill with additional "pristine" water (see above) as desired.

>>>——→ Use novelty ice trays for perfectly square ice or cubes shaped like shells, hearts, and the like (for sources, see page 140).

>>>——→ Create an ice ring for all out punch finesse. For a recipe, see page 82.

CENTERS OF ATTENTION

BEAUTIFUL AND EASY CENTERPIECE IDEAS

THE TRICK TO SETTING A BUFFET CENTERPIECE OR FOCAL POINT ON EACH TABLE IS NOT TO GO OVERBOARD WITH EXUBERANCE, BUT TO CREATE THE IMPRESSION THAT YOU'VE EFFORTLESSLY (HA!) THROWN SOME THINGS TOGETHER. KEEP IT SIMPLE— REMEMBER, YOU ARE ENTERTAINING ON A PORCH. HERE ARE SOME IDEAS.

SMALL WONDERS Enlist small vases, jars, decorative tin cans, creamers, and sugar bowls for little bouquets.

POP WITH POP Add one gerbera daisy to a variety of old bottles that, on a riser, can line the back of your buffet. Elsewhere, brown root beer bottles sporting one large white flower (think spider mum or lily) in each can be very striking.

COWBOY CHIC Pick out a pair of cowboy boots, the more colorful and worn the better. Find a vase that fits snugly inside the boots and fill with complementary wildflowers or other unfussy flowers. For smaller arrangements, or for a child's party, adopt a child's cowboy boot or boots and smaller glasses to inset.

NEAT YOUR VEGGIES Line green or white asparagus stalks or long green beans around a medium vase so that the tops of the asparagus rise about an inch over the top of the vase; trim the bottom of each stalk so it is flush to the bottom of the vase. Use clear molding putty or poster tape to adhere each spear to the glass. Secure the spears to the vase with raffia or ribbon.

FESTIVE FRUIT Find tall vases and fill with colorful lemons, limes, or cranberries. Use on their own or work in stalks of tropical cuttings such as tall flowering ginger, birds of paradise, or lilies.

NATURAL CONFETTI Use fall leaves or rose petals to elegantly set the stage for a table but be careful not to make it look like a parade or high wind has just passed through.

PEAR-FECTION A flat dish of sculptural pears is always tasteful, and the aroma they impart is a plus.

ART(ICHOKES) SHOW Line tables with low square vases filled with water and one oversize artichoke, complete with stalk, in each.

SCENTS-ABILITY Nestle candles into wide, low bowls or staggered glass votives filled with aromatic coffee beans.

NOW SEA HERE Add shells to vases to hide flower stems.

LIGHTS FANTASTIC Light hurricane lanterns, small votives, and dramatic candelabras (if it's not windy).

NAPKIN BEAUTY Use twine to bunch up a napkin and create a bow. Tuck in freshly clipped herbs (flowering ones are delightful).

YARD SALE Use what you already have. Branches (especially moss-covered ones) from small trees look gorgeous on their own in tall vases; some finer branches with offshoots are fun to adorn with small holiday ornaments. Lovely oversize leaves also can be pretty in vases, playing solo or complementing other flora and fauna.

GET NOSTALGIC Plunk wildflowers into vintage mason jars.

GOURD IDEA Hollow out pumpkins to display small mums or candles.

Just remember—keep arrangements on tables low, or at least staggered, so people easily can look at each other.

PORCH, VERANDA, GALLERY
WHAT GIVES?

You say porch, I say veranda.
BUT WHO'S RIGHT? THERE ARE INDEED DIFFERENCES, AND HERE'S THE GENERAL THINKING ON THIS SUBJECT.

VERANDA
a large, grand porch, usually open or perhaps partially screened-in.

PORCH
a smaller, more intimate space, sometimes screened-in.

GALLERY
typically an upstairs porch, or area adjoining building sections.

COLONNADE
a covered expanse with a series of columns.

STOOP
a small covered entrance at the front or back of a house; more like a platform (not a place that would afford much area to party).

CHAPTER

№ 2

WITH BAR AND RESTAURANT COCKTAIL MENUS

GETTING MORE INVENTIVE BY THE DAY, ALL TOO OFTEN WE GET STRESSED OUT OVER HAVING A TRULY IMPRESSIVE "SHOW" COCKTAIL AT A GATHERING. *WELL, MY FRIENDS, CHILL.* THESE COCKTAILS ARE HERE TO SAVE THE DAY, ER, EVENING...

CONVIVIAL COCKTAILS

APPLE
martini

With its pale gold color, smooth texture, and apple-y perfume, this martini is elegant both to sip and look at. It's a perfect offering for dressy gatherings and casual ones, too; plus, it's so easy to make.

1½ OUNCES VODKA, CHILLED

1½ OUNCES APPLE SCHNAPPS

1 TO 1½ OUNCES APPLE JUICE

GARNISH: APPLE SLICE (OPTIONAL)

Combine all ingredients except the garnish in an ice-filled cocktail shaker. Shake well and strain into a chilled martini glass. Garnish, if desired.

DO TELL:
VODKA SHOULD BE STORED IN THE FREEZER TO HELP KEEP DRINKS ICE-COLD—JUST THE WAY THEY NEED TO BE. ROOM-TEMPERATURE VODKA QUICKLY MELTS A COCKTAIL SHAKER'S ICE AND DILUTES THE DRINK. VODKA DOESN'T FREEZE BECAUSE IT IS SO HIGH IN ALCOHOL, WHICH FREEZES AT A MUCH LOWER TEMPERATURE THAN WATER. TO FREEZE AN 80-PROOF VODKA (40 PERCENT ALCOHOL), IT WOULD TAKE SETTING YOUR FREEZER DIAL TO -22 DEGREES F.

SERVES 1

blood orange
MARTINI

This seductive, deep ruby-orange drink will be beloved by those who enjoy the tartness of blood oranges; for those, like me, who prefer a little more sweetness, ring the rim with superfine sugar.

RIM: SUPERFINE SUGAR AND BLOOD ORANGE JUICE (OPTIONAL)

3 OUNCES ORANGE-FLAVORED VODKA

1 OUNCE ORANGE-FLAVORED LIQUEUR (SEE FACING PAGE)

3 OUNCES BLOOD ORANGE JUICE (SEE NOTE)

GARNISH: 2 BLOOD ORANGE SLICES OR ORANGE CURLS (OPTIONAL)

If desired, place the superfine sugar in a small shallow dish. Moisten the rims of two chilled martini glasses with the blood orange juice. Dip the rims into the sugar and set aside.

Combine the vodka, liqueur, and 3 ounces blood orange juice (strained through a fine-mesh strainer if need be) in an ice-filled cocktail shaker. Shake well and strain into the prepared martini glasses. Garnish, if desired.

NOTE: YOU CAN OFTEN FIND FRESHLY SQUEEZED BLOOD ORANGE JUICE IN GOURMET MARKETS. THE TWO MOST POPULAR VARIETIES ARE THE MORO, WITH THE DARKEST FLESH (AVAILABLE DECEMBER THROUGH MARCH), AND THE TAROCCO, LIGHTER AND MORE DELICATE IN FLAVOR (AVAILABLE JANUARY THROUGH MAY).

SERVES 2

KNOW YOUR ORANGE
LIQUEURS

TRIPLE SEC is a simple and sweet orange-flavored liqueur; at its best it's made from brandy or cognac. It's very similar to CURAÇAO ("cure-a-soh"), which distinguishes itself as being made from the dried peels of bitter oranges grown on its namesake Caribbean island. On the highest quality end of the Triple Sec scale is COINTREAU ("kwan-troh"), produced in France from a variety of bitter oranges GRAND MARNIER is a brandy-based orange liqueur that could be considered an orange-flavored cognac. Grand Marnier tends to offer richer, more full bodied orange-brandy sweetness, while Triple Sec, curaçao, and Cointreau tend to be sharper and more focused on orange peel flavor.

STRAWBERRY MARTINI

When I first enjoyed this beautiful martini, at Dallas's Sushi Samba, I thought I might swoon with happiness. This mellow-sweet, perfect-for-spring Strawberry Martini with a touch of guava was the epitome of cool. And as for the strawberry vodka? You'll definitely be hooked.

RIM: SUPERFINE SUGAR AND 1 LIME WEDGE

1 TEASPOON SUPERFINE SUGAR

2 OUNCES STRAWBERRY-FLAVORED VODKA, CHILLED

½ OUNCE TRIPLE SEC

½ OUNCE GUAVA JUICE OR NECTAR

½ OUNCE FRESH LIME JUICE

GARNISH: STRAWBERRY, SLICED HALFWAY UP (OPTIONAL)

Place the superfine sugar in a small shallow dish. Moisten the rim of a chilled martini glass with the lime wedge. Dip the rim in the sugar and set aside.

Combine the 1 teaspoon sugar, vodka, Triple Sec, guava juice, and lime juice in an ice-filled cocktail shaker. Shake well and strain into the prepared glass. Garnish, if desired.

DO TELL:
LEGENDARY WRITER H.L. MENCKEN ONCE MUSED THAT THE MARTINI WAS "THE ONLY AMERICAN INVENTION AS PERFECT AS THE SONNET."

SERVES 1

CONCORD GRAPE MARTINI

This is a crown jewel in the world of refined martinis. It's smooth, has real depth of character (thanks to the gin), and boasts a captivating deep purple hue. Grape juice with gin will be your new favorite cocktail. Trust me.

4 OUNCES GIN

3 OUNCES UNSWEETENED CONCORD GRAPE JUICE

GARNISH: CONCORD OR DARK RED GRAPE CLUSTERS TO HANG ON GLASSES (SEE NOTE; OPTIONAL)

Combine the gin and grape juice in an ice-filled cocktail shaker. Shake well and strain into chilled martini glasses. Garnish, if desired.

NOTE: CONCORD GRAPES ARE USUALLY AVAILABLE IN SEPTEMBER AND OCTOBER.

SERVES 2

GREEN TEA 'TINI

With green tea this and green tea that, little wonder that a green tea martini would emerge (but isn't that, like, an oxymoron?). Our friend Kirk Kirksey shared this with us on his porch one evening and we were swept away by the immense flavor—and soft green color—of the green tea liqueur. This gives new meaning to drinking to one's health.

3 TO 4 OUNCES CITRUS-FLAVORED
VODKA, CHILLED

2 OUNCES GREEN TEA LIQUEUR
(SEE NOTE)

1 OUNCE LEMON-LIME SODA

GARNISH: LEMON OR LIME TWISTS
(OPTIONAL)

Combine the vodka, liqueur, and soda in an ice-filled cocktail shaker. Shake well and strain into chilled martini glasses. Garnish, if desired.

NOTE: FOR SOURCES, SEE PAGE 140.

DO TELL:
GREEN TEA IS SUPPOSED TO HELP DETER BAD (LDL) CHOLESTEROL, CONTROL WEIGHT AND AID IN DIGESTION, COMBAT STRESS, AND SERVE AS AN ANTI-OXIDANT TO FIGHT CANCER AND AGING. SO WHY AREN'T WE GULPING THIS STUFF DAY AND NIGHT?

SERVES 2

best. margarita. ever.

I've no scientific proof to back this up, but I'm confident that one of the top five requested porch drinks is the margarita. That's surely true in my home state of Texas, where margaritas practically flow from fountains (and sometimes actually do). That proved a challenge when I moved to Austin in my early thrities—until I realized I'd been living in a parallel universe of tequila. You see, early on I decided I didn't like the drink. (OK, so I drank way too much of the cheap stuff one college evening; the result wasn't pretty.) Then I discovered the well-crafted stuff—a.k.a. "top-shelf" or "Cadillac" tequila, exquisitely golden, smooth, and silky. In this drink it comes with just the right amount of lime, and kick.

RIM: 1 TABLESPOON KOSHER OR
COARSE SEA SALT, ½ TEASPOON
LIME ZEST, AND 1 LIME WEDGE

2 OUNCES HIGH-QUALITY TEQUILA

1 OUNCE ORANGE-FLAVORED
LIQUEUR

1½ OUNCES FRESH LIME JUICE

GARNISH: LIME WHEEL

Combine the salt and lime zest in a small shallow dish. Moisten the rim of a margarita glass with the lime wedge. Dip the rim into the salt-zest mixture and set aside.

Combine the tequila, liqueur, and lime juice in an ice-filled cocktail shaker. Shake well and strain into the prepared glass. Garnish, if desired.

SERVES 1

minty mango
M A R G I

With margaritas elevated to new heights and flavors, this one's a personal favorite. Here, sweet and sour meet cool mango and liquid gold (tequila) with a kick of mint. The addition of fresh mango gives it more of a rustic appearance.

12 MINT LEAVES

½ FRESH MANGO, PEELED AND DIVIDED IN HALF (SEE NOTE)

4 OUNCES GOOD TEQUILA

½ OUNCE MANGO SCHNAPPS

2 OUNCES MANGO NECTAR

3 OUNCES SOUR MIX

GARNISH: MINT SPRIGS (OPTIONAL)

In each of two highball glasses, muddle the mint leaves. Add half of the mango to each glass and muddle. Add enough ice to each glass so it is three-quarters full.

In a cocktail shaker, combine the tequila, schnapps, nectar, and sour mix, and shake. Pour into each glass and stir to combine with the mint and mango. Garnish, if desired.

NOTE: OMIT THE FRESH MANGO IF YOU WANT A CRISPER, MORE TART DRINK. FOR TIPS ON CUTTING INTO A MANGO, SEE PAGE 101.

SERVES 2

BANANA DAIQUIRI

From what I've heard, this drink is purportedly Rolling Stones guitarist Keith Richards' favorite tropical beverage—a fact I adore about the rough-and-tumble rock 'n' roller (who perhaps was drinking one when he fell out of a coconut tree not long ago?).

- 6 OUNCES LIGHT RUM
- 1 OUNCE WHITE CRÈME DE CACAO
- 2 OUNCES BANANA-FLAVORED LIQUEUR
- 2 TO 3 CUPS CRUSHED ICE

- 3 BANANAS, CUT INTO THIRDS
- GARNISH: PAPER UMBRELLAS OR TIPS OF BANANAS SLICED ON THE BIAS AND SERVED ON THE RIM (OPTIONAL)

Process the rum, crème de cacao, and liqueur in a blender filled with crushed ice. When well mixed, add the bananas, and pulse until well blended. Pour into festive cocktail or martini glasses. Garnish, if desired.

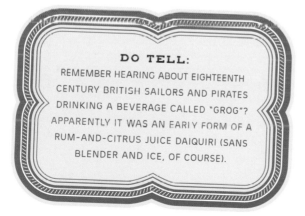

DO TELL:
REMEMBER HEARING ABOUT EIGHTEENTH CENTURY BRITISH SAILORS AND PIRATES DRINKING A BEVERAGE CALLED "GROG"? APPARENTLY IT WAS AN EARLY FORM OF A RUM-AND-CITRUS JUICE DAIQUIRI (SANS BLENDER AND ICE, OF COURSE).

SERVES 2–3

PIÑA COLADA

It's really important to know that cream of coconut is not coconut milk, as in what you'd use cooking Thai food. Cream of coconut is a thick and creamy base that gives tropical cocktails their sweet, creamy body. Canned pineapple juice is okay, but if you can buy refrigerated, do it—it has much less tang. Also, lighter rum allows more fruit flavor to show through; the darker rum tastes more rummy and pungent (and, by the way, dark rum really doesn't affect the drink's light color). Beyond those key points, find some kitschy tropical glasses to serve this in; many can be found online.

2 OUNCES CREAM OF COCONUT
(SEE NOTE)

2 OUNCES FRESH OR REFRIGERATED
PINEAPPLE JUICE

1½ OUNCES LIGHT OR DARK RUM

1 CUP CRUSHED ICE

GARNISH: PINEAPPLE WEDGE, COCKTAIL
UMBRELLA (OPTIONAL)

Process the cream of coconut, pineapple juice, rum, and ice in a blender until smooth. Pour into a cocktail glass with a straw. Garnish, if desired.

NOTE: MOST LIQUOR STORES CARRY THIS, BUT FOR A SOURCE, SEE PAGE 140.

SERVES 1

SUBLIME
CUBA LIBRE

I'm sure my adoration for this drink—essentially a rum 'n' Coke—stems from a trip to Puerto Vallarta. I'll never forget the beauty of dining on the covered patio of a hacienda-restaurant, with a mariachi band playing the Beatles' "Norwegian Wood" to accompany a glorious sunset (and those of us singing along—gleefully thanks to the Cuba Libres we were drinking). I swore I would never have another one of these without making them just as the bartender did that evening—with lots of amber rum and lime wedges.

2 OUNCES AMBER OR WHITE RUM
(SEE NOTE)

2 OUNCES COCA-COLA, CHILLED

4 LIME WEDGES

GARNISH: LIME WEDGES (OPTIONAL)

In a highball glass filled with ice, pour in the rum and cola. Squeeze and drop in the lime wedges, and, using a bar spoon, stir to mix well. Garnish, if desired.

DO TELL:
THIS DRINK, SPANISH FOR "FREE CUBA," MOST LIKELY COMES FROM EX-CUBAN PATRIOTS OF THE SPANISH-AMERICAN WAR HAILING THEIR NATIVE COUNTRY IN THE YEARS FOLLOWING THE WAR (AROUND THE TIME OF COCA-COLA'S INVENTION IN 1900).

NOTE: FOR TESTING PURPOSES, I USED WHAT I ENJOYED THAT FINE EVENING: APPLETON ESTATE JAMAICA RUM.

SERVES 1

PROSECCO MOJITO

It makes perfect sense that one fizzy—club soda—could be replaced by an even nicer one—sparkling Prosecco. You'll love the topaz color the brown sugar imparts. For a nonalcoholic version of this drink, see the Nojito (page 112).

5 MINT LEAVES

1 TEASPOON BROWN SUGAR

½ OUNCE SIMPLE SYRUP (PAGE 26)

½ OUNCE FRESH LIME JUICE

2 OUNCES LIGHT RUM

2 OUNCES PROSECCO (SPARKLING WINE OR CHAMPAGNE)

GARNISH: MINT SPRIG (OPTIONAL)

In a pilsner or highball glass, muddle the mint leaves with the brown sugar, simple syrup, and lime juice. Add ice cubes. Pour in the rum and top with the Prosecco. Stir. Garnish, if desired.

DO TELL:
PROSECCO—LEMONY, DRY, AND SPARKLING IS MADE WITH WHITE GRAPES FROM ITALY'S VENETO REGION, WHICH IS IN THE FOOTHILLS OF THE ALPS.

SERVES 1

GUMBY
SLUMBER

My friend Elizabeth Harrell knows a thing or three about porch entertaining; her 1920s Tampa home has one of Hyde Park's most hospitable verandas. That's even more true when she's serving her favorite drink from Little Palm Island Resort & Spa, midway between Key Largo and Key West. The drink was named by one of the resort's earliest bartenders, who noticed how the concoction leaves guests in a Gumbylike (pliable) state, desirous to slumber in a hammock. Consider this a massage in a glass.

1½ OUNCES PINEAPPLE JUICE

1½ OUNCES CRANBERRY JUICE

1½ OUNCES ORANGE JUICE

1½ OUNCES SPICED RUM (SEE NOTE)

1½ OUNCES COCONUT-FLAVORED OR WHITE RUM (SEE NOTE)

GARNISH: PINEAPPLE SLICE (OPTIONAL)

Combine the juices and rums in an ice-filled cocktail shaker. Shake well and strain into a highball glass filled with ice. Garnish, if desired.

NOTE: LITTLE PALM ISLAND RESORT & SPA USES CAPTAIN MORGAN SPICED RUM AND CAPTAIN MORGAN PARROT BAY RUM.

DO TELL: HAMMOCKS WERE DESIGNED BY EARLY LATIN AMERICANS TO KEEP THEMSELVES SAFE FROM SNAKES, INSECTS, AND MUD AND WATER WHEN IT RAINED.

SERVES 1

BRUNCH BLOODY MARY

This drink is synonymous with porch-side relaxation and early weekend brunches. Making it fresh is much better than using prefab mixes, which lean toward the salty, preservative-y side. Plus, seeing all the ingredients swirl hither and yon within the glass is a delight.

RIM: 2 TABLESPOONS OLD BAY SEASONING AND LIME WEDGE

1 CUP TOMATO JUICE, CHILLED

1 OUNCE VODKA, CHILLED

½ OUNCE FRESH LIME OR LEMON JUICE

1 TEASPOON WORCESTERSHIRE SAUCE

5 DROPS HOT SAUCE

½ TEASPOON PREPARED HORSERADISH

¼ TEASPOON CELERY SALT

GARNISH: CELERY STALK, PICKLED GREEN BEAN, OKRA POD, OR BANANA PEPPER (OPTIONAL)

Place the seasoning in a small shallow dish. Moisten the rim of a cocktail or highball glass with the lime wedge. Dip the rim in the seasoning and set aside.

Add ice to the prepared glass. Add all ingredients except the garnish and stir well. Garnish, if desired.

DO TELL:

THOUGH THE BLOODY MARY IS BELIEVED BY MANY TO BE A NOD TO THE UNFORTUNATE NICKNAME OF QUEEN MARY I OF ENGLAND, MANY COCKTAIL HISTORIANS THINK THE DRINK'S CREATOR, COMEDIC ACTOR GEORGE JESSEL (1898–1981), MORE LIKELY HAD LEGENDARY ACTRESS MARY PICKFORD IN MIND. SHE REPORTEDLY ENJOYED A SIMILAR DEEP RED "BLOODY" DRINK MADE WITH RUM, GRENADINE, AND MARASCHINO CHERRY JUICE.

SERVES 1

pear mimosa

Pear nectar is much smoother than orange juice and makes for a delicious twist on the standard mimosa. Try this for a dressy porch-side reception.

ONE 750-MILLILITER BOTTLE
CHAMPAGNE OR SPARKLING WINE,
CHILLED (SEE NOTE)

2 CUPS PEAR NECTAR, CHILLED

GARNISH: MINT SPRIGS (OPTIONAL)

Combine the sparkling wine and nectar in large pitcher; keep chilled.

Pour into Champagne flutes. Garnish, if desired.

NOTE: SUBSTITUTE SPARKLING WHITE GRAPE JUICE FOR THOSE WHO MIGHT NOT ENJOY TRADITIONAL BUBBLY.

DO TELL:
IF YOU FEEL LIKE YOU'RE PUTTIN' ON THE RITZ WHILE DRINKING THIS, IN ESSENCE, YOU ARE. THE MIMOSA COCKTAIL WAS REPORTEDLY INVENTED AROUND 1925 AT THE RITZ HOTEL IN PARIS.

SERVES 4

TIPSY TEA

with HOMEMADE SWEET TEA

Sweet tea never tasted so good—especially for those bent on unwinding after a long workweek. Try it with a lunch of fried chicken and deviled eggs and see if you don't agree.

2 OUNCES ORANGE-FLAVORED VODKA, CHILLED

6 OUNCES SWEET TEA (RECIPE FOLLOWS), CHILLED

GARNISH: ½ ORANGE WHEEL (OPTIONAL)

Add the vodka and tea to a tall glass filled with ice; stir well. Garnish, if desired.

SWEET TEA

10 CUPS COLD WATER

2 FAMILY-SIZE OR 8 REGULAR BLACK TEA BAGS

¾ CUP SUGAR

Boil 3 cups of the water, then add the tea bags; continue boiling for 1 minute. Cover and set aside to steep for about 15 minutes.

Remove and discard the tea bags. Add the sugar, stirring to dissolve.

Pour the tea mixture into a 1-gallon container, then add the remaining 7 cups cold water. Stir to combine.

MAKES 2½ QUARTS

SERVES 1

WATERMELON COOLER

This is the dreamiest drink I've had in ages. So agree the friends I most recently shared it with. They, like me, love how it's naturally sweetened with honey. It's a lot of fun to serve in chilled jelly glasses.

4 CUPS 2-INCH CUBES WATERMELON	2 TABLESPOONS HONEY (SEE NOTE)
1 CUP VODKA, CHILLED	GARNISH: SMALL WATERMELON WEDGES WITH RIND (OPTIONAL)

Freeze the watermelon chunks in a zip-top plastic bag until just frozen, about 1 hour. Remove from the freezer and add to a blender. Pour in the vodka and honey.

Process until blended and pour into frosted cocktail or jelly glasses. Garnish, if desired.

NOTE: USE STANDARD HONEY (SAY, CLOVER) INSTEAD OF A DARK OR OTHER STRONGLY FLAVORED VERSION; OTHERWISE IT'LL CHANGE THE DRINK'S FLAVOR IN A DISAPPOINTING WAY.

DO TELL: THE YOUNG, SOFT WHITE SEEDS IN A "SEEDLESS" WATERMELON ARE PERFECTLY FINE TO INGEST. ACTUALLY, THEY MAKE YOUR DRINK LOOK EVEN MORE WATERMELON-Y.

SERVES 4

BLACKBERRY SMASH

I love the fact that I discovered this drink at a Dallas restaurant named the Porch. Indeed, the drink is a perfect porch-crowd pleaser. You'll love the wonderful marriage of mint and blackberry, and its gorgeous deep ruby color.

10 FRESH MINT LEAVES

16 FRESH BLACKBERRIES (SEE NOTE)

½ CUP RYE WHISKEY

1 TABLESPOON FRESH LEMON JUICE

2 TABLESPOONS SIMPLE SYRUP (PAGE 26)

½ CUP GINGER ALE, PLUS MORE FOR TOPPING OFF

GARNISH: SKEWERS OF FRESH BLACKBERRIES (OPTIONAL)

Muddle the mint and blackberries in a cocktail shaker. Add the whiskey, lemon juice, simple syrup, and ½ cup ginger ale. Add ice and mix with bar spoon (don't shake—remember there's ginger ale in there). Pour into wide-mouth or tall cocktail glasses filled with ice. Top off with extra ginger ale to taste. Garnish, if desired.

NOTE: ONE 16-OUNCE CONTAINER EQUALS ENOUGH BLACKBERRIES FOR DRINK AND GARNISHES.

SERVES 2

POMEGRANATE
PIMM'S CUP

As if the Pimm's Cup wasn't already one of the most refreshing cocktails ever, here's a version that uses pomegranate juice, which really takes the herbaceous Pimm's liqueur to the next level. The drink's distinctive aroma and beautiful garnet color gives it royal flair. A sunken cucumber lends the ultimate freshness.

1½ OUNCES PIMM'S NO. 1 LIQUEUR

2 OUNCES CHILLED POMEGRANATE-
CHERRY JUICE OR OTHER
SWEETENED POMEGRANATE JUICE

GINGER ALE OR LEMON-LIME SODA

GARNISH: CUCUMBER SLICE (OPTIONAL)

Pour the Pimm's liqueur and pomegranate juice into a cocktail glass filled with ice. Top off with ginger ale and stir. Garnish, if desired.

DO TELL:

PIMM'S NO. 1 IS MADE WITH A SECRET
LIQUEUR RECIPE OF DRY GIN, FRUIT JUICES, AND
SPICES. CREATED BY ENGLISH OYSTER BAR OWNER
JAMES PIMM IN THE EARLY NINETEENTH CENTURY, THE
DRINK WAS MEANT TO BE A TONIC SERVED IN A
SMALL ("NO. 1" SIZE) CUP TO AID DIGESTION.

SERVES 1

MICHELADA

Whenever I sip this with new friends, I usually share a funny story about a trip we once took to Oaxaca, Mexico. While sipping *micheladas* at a café near the *zocalo* (main square), our group became the target of a kooky resident intent on "scanning" us with his homemade Geiger counter. Fortunately we didn't register anything alarming. But what *did* register with us was how happy our drinks—beer's homage to the bloody Mary—were making us.

RIM: 2 TABLESPOONS KOSHER OR COARSE SEA SALT, 2 TABLESPOONS SALT-FREE CHILE POWDER (SEE NOTE), AND 1 LIME WEDGE

2 OUNCES FRESH LIME JUICE

HOT SAUCE

SOY SAUCE

FOUR 12-OUNCE BOTTLES OF MEXICAN BEER (SEE NOTE)

LIME WEDGES FOR ADDED FLAVOR AND GARNISH

Combine the salt and chile powder in a small shallow dish. Moisten the rims of four pilsner glasses or beer mugs with the lime wedge. Dip the rims into the chile salt and set aside.

Add ½ ounce lime juice to each glass, and fill with ice about halfway. Add a dash or two of hot sauce and soy sauce to each glass and top off with the beer. Add more lime wedges as desired.

NOTE: NEW MEXICO'S CHIMAYO CHILE POWDER'S DEEP RED COLOR, EARTHY FLAVOR, AND MEDIUM HEAT PROVES JUST RIGHT (AND THE DRINK ENDS UP NOT TOO SALTY). YOU CAN OFTEN FIND IT IN GOURMET MARKETS, BUT FOR AN ONLINE SOURCE, SEE PAGE 140. DARK MEXICAN BEER (SUCH AS NEGRA MODELO) MAKES THE DRINK DENSER. LIGHTER BEER ADDS EFFERVESCENCE.

SERVES 4

PEPPERMINT TWIST

What a fun alternative to eggnog, or a refreshing after-dinner drink. It's like creamy, chilly liquid peppermint. Yum.

2 OUNCES PEPPERMINT SCHNAPPS

3 OUNCES CRÈME DE CACAO

3 OUNCES HALF-AND-HALF

GARNISH: MINT CHOCOLATE SHAVINGS OR FINELY GROUND PEPPERMINTS (OPTIONAL)

Combine the schnapps, crème de cacao, and half-and-half in an ice-filled cocktail shaker. Shake well and strain into chilled Champagne flutes. Garnish, if desired.

DO TELL:
THIS DRINK PLAYS OFF JOEY DEE AND THE STARLIGHTERS' NO. 1 SONG OF 1962, WHICH WAS A TRIBUTE TO BOTH CHUBBY CHECKER'S ICONIC SONG AND NEW YORK'S PEPPERMINT LOUNGE, WHERE THE "PEPPERMINT TWIST" DANCE CRAZE WAS CELEBRATED.

SERVES 2

BELLINI

This drink, with little bits of peach peeking through, is one of the prettiest and easiest recipes you can make for a crowd. I shortened the usual Bellini process by incorporating the Champagne into the peach puree. But for the fizziest presentation, only puree the peaches with the nectar and sugar and let that chill; fill a Champagne flute halfway with the mixture and top with Champagne.

4 CUPS FROZEN PEACHES, SLIGHTLY THAWED (SEE NOTE)

TWO 11.5-OUNCE CANS PEACH NECTAR

1 CUP SUPERFINE SUGAR (SEE NOTE)

ONE 750-MILLILITER BOTTLE CHAMPAGNE OR SPARKLING WINE

CRUSHED ICE (OPTIONAL)

GARNISH: MINT SPRIGS (OPTIONAL)

Process half of the peaches, nectar, sugar, and sparkling wine in a blender until smooth, stopping to scrape down the sides and ensure the peaches get well pureed. Repeat with the remaining peaches, nectar, sugar, and sparkling wine. Refrigerate. Pour into Champagne flutes or wine goblets half-filled with crushed ice, if desired. Garnish, if desired.

NOTE: YOU CAN USE FRESH PEACHES BUT TO SAVE TIME AND GET THE BEST CHILL FACTOR, GO WITH FROZEN—THEY'RE REALLY JUST AS GOOD. GRANULATED SUGAR WILL WORK BUT IT WON'T INCORPORATE AS WELL; YOU'LL NEED TO STIR IT A BIT MORE AS YOU'RE SERVING. THIS COULD ALSO BE NICE IN A NONALCOHOLIC VERSION USING SPARKLING PEACH JUICE.

DO TELL: THE BELLINI WAS FIRST INVENTED IN 1948 AT HARRY'S BAR IN VENICE, ITALY. THE DRINK WAS NAMED AFTER FIFTEENTH CENTURY PAINTER GIOVANNI BELLINI.

SERVES 10

PITCHER
❖ OF ❖
JULEPS

Stanley Dry is a real inspiration. The Louisiana native chose to leave the intoxicating swirl of being a food editor for *Food & Wine* in New York City for a more enviable position in New Iberia, Louisiana, where he works the land (his garden, actually). He also figured out how to make the easiest batch of mint juleps you'll ever meet. Do know that these juleps are minty-sweet, which is indeed wonderful but a bit deceptive—you may not realize how powerful the bourbon-y elixir is.

2 CUPS WATER

¾ CUP SUGAR

3 CUPS LOOSELY PACKED MINT LEAVES

2 CUPS BOURBON

GARNISH: FRESH MINT SPRIGS (OPTIONAL)

Combine the water and sugar in a medium saucepan over medium heat; stir until the sugar dissolves. Add the mint and bring to a boil. Remove from the heat, cover, and let steep at least 30 minutes.

Strain mint syrup through a fine-mesh sieve or coffee filter and let cool. Combine with the bourbon in a sealable container. Keep well chilled.

Transfer the julep to a serving pitcher. Pour into cocktail or julep cups filled with ice. Garnish, if desired.

SERVES 8

RUBY
Sangria

I've become infatuated with apothecary-style beverage urns fitted with spigots, since they are especially beautiful for presenting fruited drinks. Sangria is the ultimate example. Not only can you see the bounty of fruit flavoring the wine mixture inside, but you also can tap into the drink's full flavor without having wimped-out fruit floating around in your glass. Serving kebobs of extra fruit lets you enjoy both the drink and the fruit at their finest.

ONE 750-MILLILITER BOTTLE
   RED WINE

½ CUP BRANDY

½ CUP ORANGE-FLAVORED LIQUEUR

½ CUP FRESH ORANGE JUICE

¼ CUP SUGAR

2 CUPS ORANGE WEDGES

2 CUPS RED APPLE WEDGES

2 CUPS GREEN APPLE WEDGES

2 CUPS GRAPES

ONE 750-MILLILITER BOTTLE
   SPARKLING WATER, CHILLED

GARNISH: GRAPES AND ORANGE WEDGES,
   RED AND GREEN APPLE WEDGES
   (ABOUT 1 CUP EACH) THREADED ON
   SMALL WOODEN SKEWERS
   (OPTIONAL)

Combine the red wine, brandy, liqueur, orange juice, and sugar in a large pitcher or plastic container; stir well. Add the oranges, red and green apples, and grapes. Chill for several hours.

Just before serving, add the sparkling water.

Pour the sangria into red-wine goblets or cocktail glasses filled with ice. Garnish with fruit kabobs, if desired.

SERVES 6–8

DESTINATION PORCHES
THE TOP FIVE

SOME PORCHES ARE CELEBRITIES IN THEIR OWN RIGHT.
HERE ARE FIVE VENERABLE ENTERTAINERS—FROM CALIFORNIA TO MAINE—
YOU SHOULDN'T MISS.

CALIFORNIA: **Hotel Del Coronado**, near San Diego. The sprawling, red-roofed, crisp-white exterior and dark wood-paneled lobby may look 1888, when the Hotel Del (as fans like to call it) first opened on the beach. Or it might bring back memories of the movie *Some Like It Hot*, which was filmed there. But everything else about the place—its room decor, its spa, its well-tended porches—is very now. 800-468-3533 or HotelDel.com.

MAINE: **Grey Havens Inn, Georgetown Island**. Since 1904 this cedar-shingled, turreted gem has been offering a 180-degree view of midcoast Maine's rocky bay, which reaches to the Atlantic. The porch, half of it screened, envelops the old-fashioned, family-run inn on three sides. Open seasonally. 800-431-2316 or GreyHavens.com.

MICHIGAN: **Grand Hotel, Macinac Island**. First, the pronunciation: It's "mack-in-awe." Next, another pronouncement: built in 1867, the 385-room hotel is as old-fashioned as they come (you still have to dress up for dinner). FYI: Its 660-foot porch is the world's longest, and you can see it in the movie, *Somewhere in Time*. 800-334-7263 or GrandHotel.com.

MISSISSIPPI: Dunleith Plantation, Natchez. This stately 1856 Greek Revival manse and inn is surrounded by a two-story white colonnade overlooking 40 acres of well-tended landscape beauty not far from the Mississippi River. Grab a mint julep in the Castle Restaurant's downstairs pub—a late-18th-century Gothic-style carriage house. 800-433-2445 or Dunleith.com.

NORTH CAROLINA: The Grove Park Inn Resort & Spa, Asheville. With its signature undulating red-tile roof and impressive collection of Arts and Crafts furnishings, this is a stone mountain lodge extraordinaire, offering fabulous views of the Blue Ridge Mountains. Its partially enclosed sunset terrace is one of my favorite places to chill. Fittingly, the original owner/builder of the 1913 building was St. Louis entrepreneur E. W. Grove, who made a fortune peddling "Grove's Tasteless Chill Tonic." 800-438-5800 or GroveParkInn.com.

Left To Right: HOTEL DEL CORONADO; GRAND HOTEL, MACINAC ISLAND; DUNLEITH PLANTATION

CHAPTER

N⁰

HERE'S WHAT WE KNOW ABOUT PUNCH:

(1) PUNCH IS COOL AGAIN.

(2) PUNCH IS THOUGHT TO BE SHORT FOR "PUNCHEON," AN OLD ENGLISH WORD FOR A WINE CASK THAT HELD 72 GALLONS.

(3) PUNCH SHOULD HAVE AT LEAST THREE BUT PREFERABLY FIVE INGREDIENTS AND SERVE A BOATLOAD OF PEOPLE (OR AT LEAST A SMALL CROWD).

(4) THESE FESTIVE CONCOCTIONS, WITH ALCOHOL AND WITHOUT, ARE JUST WHAT YOU NEED TO PUNCH UP YOUR PARTY.

PUNCH with PIZZAZZ

BLUSH
PUNCH

Punch doesn't always have to be served in traditional punch cups. Consider the occasion—for more traditional gatherings, certainly enlist your heirloom cups, but for more modern-minded parties, think of using distinctive Champagne flutes.

ONE 12-OUNCE CONTAINER FROZEN PINK LEMONADE CONCENTRATE, THAWED

4 CUPS CRANBERRY JUICE COCKTAIL (SEE NOTE)

4 CUPS CLUB SODA, CHILLED

GARNISH: LEMON CURLS (OPTIONAL)

Combine the pink lemonade concentrate and cranberry juice cocktail in a large pitcher or container. Stir in the club soda just before serving. Pour into Champagne flutes. Garnish, if desired.

NOTE: FOR A PALER PINK PUNCH, USE WHITE CRANBERRY JUICE COCKTAIL.

SERVES 8–10

HIBISCUS PUNCH

This makes an unexpected drink to serve porch-side visitors. With its beautiful color and sweet-tart cranberrylike flavor, guests will want to know where you had to go to find hibiscus pods, how interesting (and easy) it was to make, and talk about the sheer fact that hibiscus is edible. Be aware that with its deep red coloring, you shouldn't use a light-colored tablecloth.

4 QUARTS WATER

2 CUPS DRIED HIBISCUS FLOWER PODS (SEE NOTE)

2 CUPS SUPERFINE SUGAR

GARNISH: FRESH HIBISCUS PODS FOR PUNCH CUPS OR HIBISCUS FLOWERS TO FLOAT IN PUNCH BOWL (OPTIONAL)

Add the water and dried hibiscus to a large nonaluminum Dutch oven. Cover and let stand at least 2 hours.

Uncover the pot and bring to a boil. Reduce the heat and let simmer for 6 to 8 minutes.

Strain through a sieve, discarding the solids. Add the sugar and stir until it dissolves. Refrigerate until well chilled.

Pour into small cocktail glasses filled with ice. Garnish, if desired.

NOTE: HIBISCUS PODS OR DRIED FLOWERS ARE KNOWN AS *JAMAICA* ("HA-MYEE-KAH") IN MEXICAN AND CARIBBEAN MARKETS. FOR AN ONLINE SOURCE, SEE PAGE 140.

DO TELL: HIBISCUS—OFTEN USED TO MAKE JAMS, JELLIES, AND SAUCES—IS RICH IN VITAMIN C.

SERVES 12–14

THINK OUTSIDE THE PUNCH BOWL
PUNCH SERVERS

YES, THERE'S ALWAYS AUNT HATTIE'S CRYSTAL PUNCH BOWL, THE ONE YOU'VE KEPT IN THE ATTIC BECAUSE YOUR KITCHEN HASN'T THE ROOM TO STORE SUCH A BEHEMOTH AND ALL ITS COMPONENTS. BUT UNLESS YOU'RE THROWING A FULL-SCALE BRIDAL SHOWER OR WEDDING PARTY, THERE ARE OTHER, MORE CREATIVE OPTIONS TO CONSIDER.

⫸→ Vintage aluminum stew pot with complementary ladle and cups

⫸→ Carved-out large watermelon (skillful sorts can even craft a handle of a melon "basket")

⫸→ Large decorative pitcher(s)

⫸→ Large decorative urn or trophy with antique silver punch ladle

⫸→ Big plastic bowl fitted within a large round basket (with flowers, greenery, or fabric filling the gap)

⫸→ Mexican *agua fresca* jar with ladle (for sources, see page 140)

⫸→ Old pickle jar with ladle

⫸→ Fun and retro insulated aluminum watercooler

⫸→ Large glass jar with spigot

⫸→ Very clean vintage porcelain baby bath vessel (having floating toy ducks in it would be especially fun for a baby shower)

lemon Sherbet
PUNCH

This refresher can be made in a pinch and looks lovely in a punch bowl, especially with thin lemon slices floating on top.

2 QUARTS (64 OUNCES) LEMON SHERBET

ONE 2-LITER BOTTLE LEMON-LIME SODA OR GINGER ALE (SEE NOTE)

ONE 12-OUNCE CONTAINER FROZEN LEMONADE CONCENTRATE, THAWED

GARNISH: LEMON SLICES (OPTIONAL)

Combine the sherbet, soda, and lemonade concentrate in a large punch bowl. Using a wire whisk, mash the sherbet into and along the sides of the bowl to fully incorporate it into the liquids. Add crushed ice and garnish, if desired. Pour into punch cups.

NOTE: IF YOU WANT A TARTER, MORE YELLOW PUNCH, GO FOR THE LEMON-LIME SODA; FOR A GINGERY FLAVOR AND TONED-DOWN YELLOW, GO WITH THE GINGER ALE.

A
TASTEFUL

TO HELP GET SHERBET OUT OF ITS CONTAINER, TURN IT OVER IN THE PUNCH BOWL. RINSE A KITCHEN TOWEL IN HOT WATER AND WRING OUT MOST OF THE WATER. PLACE THE TOWEL ATOP THE CONTAINER AND LET SIT FOR SEVERAL MINUTES. REMOVE THE TOWEL AND GENTLY SQUEEZE THE SHERBET OUT OF ITS CONTAINER.

TIP

SERVES 14–16

Ice Ring Finesse

Crushed ice or ice cubes are fine in a punch, BUT TO MAKE THE PRESENTATION EVEN MORE DRAMATIC, USE THIS COLORFUL AND FRUITY ICE RING.

Fruited Ice Ring

- 1½ TO 2 CUPS FRESH ORANGE JUICE
- ½ CUP CRANBERRY JUICE
- 7 TO 8 SEEDLESS RED GRAPE CLUSTERS (FIVE OR SIX GRAPES IN EACH CLUSTER)
- 10 TO 12 ORANGE SLICES, SEEDS REMOVED
- 8 TO 10 WHOLE STRAWBERRIES
- MINT SPRIGS

Mix the juices in a small container; set aside.

Line the bottom of a 6-cup ring mold with the grape clusters and half of the orange slices, using the grape clusters as a base for the orange slices. Pour half of the juices into the mold and freeze until set.

Place the remaining orange slices, the strawberries, and mint sprigs into the mold and top with the remaining juice mixture. Let freeze overnight.

To remove the ice mold, place the bottom part of the mold into a pan of warm water for 8 to 10 seconds to loosen; repeat as necessary (using a warm towel atop the mold to help loosen). Invert onto a plate and slip into the punch of your choice.

MAKES 1 ICE RING (ABOUT 3 INCHES BY 9½ INCHES)

CLASSIC
WEDDING PUNCH

This is the tangy, sparkling punch most people are accustomed to when they think of Champagne or holiday punch.

ONE 11.5-OUNCE CONTAINER FROZEN
PINEAPPLE-ORANGE JUICE
CONCENTRATE, THAWED

ONE 6-OUNCE CONTAINER FROZEN
LEMONADE CONCENTRATE, THAWED

1½ CUPS (12 OUNCES) GINGER ALE

ONE 750-MILLILITER BOTTLE
CHAMPAGNE OR SPARKLING WINE
(SEE NOTE)

2 CUPS BOTTLED SPARKLING WATER

GARNISH: FRUITED ICE RING (FACING PAGE;
OPTIONAL)

Combine the fruit concentrate, ginger ale, Champagne, and sparkling water in a large punch bowl, stirring gently. Garnish, if desired. Serve immediately in punch cups or Champagne flutes.

NOTE: SUBSTITUTE NONALCOHOLIC SPARKLING OR STILL WHITE GRAPE JUICE IF DESIRED.

"AT THE PUNCH-BOWL'S BRINK,
LET THE THIRSTY THINK,
WHAT THEY SAY IN JAPAN:
FIRST THE MAN TAKES A DRINK,
THEN THE DRINK TAKES A DRINK,
THEN THE DRINK TAKES THE MAN."

— U.S. POET EDWARD ROWLAND SILL
(1841–1887) IN "AN ADAGE FROM THE ORIENT"

SERVES 10–12

VERY GOOD
champagne punch

I say "very good" here because this is top-of-the-line punch, with brandy and orange liqueur giving it star power. Think of it as a Champagne cosmopolitan.

ONE 750-MILLILITER BOTTLE CHAMPAGNE OR SPARKLING WINE

2 OUNCES GRENADINE

3 OUNCES ORANGE-FLAVORED LIQUEUR (SEE PAGE 37)

2 OUNCES BRANDY

GARNISH: ORANGE RIND SLIVERS (OPTIONAL)

Combine the Champagne, grenadine, liqueur, and brandy in a pitcher and mix well. Chill for at least 1 hour.

Pour into Champagne glasses filled with crushed or cracked ice. Garnish, if desired.

DO TELL:

WHY DOES CHAMPAGNE GIVE PEOPLE A HEADACHE? WELL, NOT ALL OF IT DOES. THE CHEAPER-QUALITY ONES EMPLOY TOO MUCH SUGAR, AND WHEN USED IN VERY SWEET PUNCHES, THAT CAN DO ANYBODY IN (ESPECIALLY IF THEY JUST SIMPLY DRINK TOO MUCH). THE DRIER THE CHAMPAGNE OR SPARKLING WINE, THE BETTER.

SERVES 4–6

CAPE COD PUNCH

Call it laziness, but it's really nice not to play bartender all night. That's why I love this super-refreshing drink, typically served as a cocktail, presented as a punch. Set up the bowl and let everyone divide and conquer.

ONE 48-OUNCE BOTTLE CRANBERRY JUICE COCKTAIL

1½ CUPS CRANBERRY-FLAVORED OR UNFLAVORED VODKA, CHILLED

½ CUP SWEETENED LIME JUICE (SUCH AS ROSE'S)

ONE 1-LITER BOTTLE GINGER ALE, CHILLED

GARNISH: FRESH CRANBERRIES AND LIME WEDGES ON SKEWERS (OPTIONAL)

Combine the cranberry juice cocktail, vodka, sweetened lime juice, and ginger ale in a large serving container. Chill for several hours. Serve in cocktail glasses filled with ice. Garnish, if desired.

A TASTEFUL TIP: IF YOU PLAN TO SERVE THIS DRINK IN A PUNCH BOWL, FOLLOW THE FRUITED ICE RING RECIPE (PAGE 82), USING FRESH CRANBERRIES AND LIME SLICES FOR THE FRUIT. AS A DECOR IDEA, FILL A CLEAR GLASS VASE HALFWAY TO TWO-THIRDS UP WITH FRESH CRANBERRIES. SLOWLY POUR IN WATER UNTIL IT REACHES THE BASE OF THE TOP ROW OF CRANBERRIES. (DON'T TRY TO ADD CRANBERRIES AFTER YOU'VE ADDED WATER OR THEY'LL FLOAT AND NOT STAY SETTLED.) WORK IN STEMS OF FRESH FLOWERS AS DESIRED: GREEN AND/OR WHITE ONES, FOR EXAMPLE, PLAY WELL DURING THE HOLIDAYS.

SERVES 10–12

RUM YUM
PUNCH

During a trip to Negril, Jamaica—where I proceeded to occupy almost every hammock I found—I wrote down the basic ingredients of this drink on a bar's cocktail napkin (which I kept stuck in my "to do" folder until I began working on this book). I shall now throw away the smeared, shredded scribbling—but not the blissful memory of drinking it to the sound of soft reggae music and waves.

2½ CUPS ORANGE JUICE

2½ CUPS FRESH PINEAPPLE JUICE

⅛ CUP FRESH LIME JUICE

1¼ CUPS COCONUT-FLAVORED RUM

½ CUP DARK RUM

3 TABLESPOONS GRENADINE

GARNISH: ORANGE WHEELS OR PINEAPPLE WEDGES (OPTIONAL)

Combine the fruit juices, rums, and grenadine in a large pitcher. Pour into medium or tall cocktail glasses filled with ice. Garnish, if desired.

SERVES 8

natchez
MILK PUNCH

My Mississippi River hometown of Natchez, a few hours north of New Orleans, is known for its antebellum houses, its Southern hospitality, and the truly fine milk punch you're apt to enjoy there. This is my family's recipe, which you can double for a crowd. Serve it very cold.

2 CUPS HALF-AND-HALF

2 CUPS MILK

1½ CUPS BRANDY

1½ TEASPOONS VANILLA EXTRACT

GARNISH: GROUND NUTMEG

Combine the half-and-half, milk, brandy, and vanilla in a pitcher. Chill for several hours or overnight.

Pour the milk punch into small cocktail glasses filled with crushed or cracked ice. Garnish with several dashes of ground nutmeg.

> A TASTEFUL TIP:
> CONSIDER DOING WHAT MANY NATCHEZIANS DO:
> TAKE MILK PUNCH TO FRIENDS AS A GIFT ON
> CHRISTMAS EVE SO THEIR FAMILIES AND VISITING
> GUESTS CAN ENJOY IT ON CHRISTMAS DAY.

SERVES 6

BOURBON SLUSH

One thing I cherish about this recipe is that it can be made a day in advance. It thaws beautifully in the punch bowl, making a slush of its own, but I add crushed ice. But what I really love is drinking the bold, citrusy cooler on the screen porch of friend Julie Martin Sunich and her husband, Michael.

6 CUPS WATER

2 CUPS STRONG TEA (RECIPE FOLLOWS)

2 CUPS BOURBON

1 CUP SUGAR

ONE 6-OUNCE CONTAINER FROZEN ORANGE JUICE CONCENTRATE, THAWED

ONE 12-OUNCE CONTAINER FROZEN LEMON JUICE CONCENTRATE, THAWED

GARNISH: MINT SPRIGS OR LEMON SLICES (OPTIONAL)

Combine the water, tea, bourbon, sugar, orange and lemon juice concentrate in a large container or bowl and mix until sugar dissolves. Pour into two gallon-size freezer bags. Freeze until an hour before serving. Place the frozen punch in a large bowl and let thaw, breaking up every 15 minutes. When punch is melted, add more ice or water as desired. Serve in punch cups. Garnish, if desired.

STRONG TEA

2 CUPS WATER

1 FAMILY-SIZE OR 4 REGULAR TEA BAGS

Boil the water. Add the tea bag(s) and let steep until cool. Discard the tea bag(s) and set aside.

MAKES 2 CUPS

SERVES 16–18

CHAPTER

N⁰ 4

SAY "FROCKTAILS" AND NOT "MOCKTAILS"

BECAUSE THERE'S NOTHING TO MOCK ABOUT PEOPLE WANTING TO HIT THE PARTY DECK WITHOUT *TRULY* HITTING THE DECK. AND I SAY "FROCKTAILS" BECAUSE THESE NONALCOHOLIC BEVERAGES ARE DOLLED UP IN BOTH DRESS AND INGREDIENTS. THE SAME GOES FOR SOME OF THE PUNCH RECIPES IN THE PRECEDING CHAPTER. OF COURSE, YOU *CAN* SPIKE THEM...

THINK FROCKTAILS NOT MOCKTAILS

AGUA FRESCA
✦ DE ✦
HONEYDEW

Agua fresca, meaning "fresh cold water" in Spanish, is truly one of the coolest drinks you can enjoy. The icy fruit drinks are most often served in one of the tall, rippled glass jars (see sources, page 140) that you see in taquerias—jars that make a great centerpiece for a party (and I just had to have one). This recipe serves a crowd, but can easily be divided in half for a smaller group.

10 CUPS PEELED HONEYDEW MELON CHUNKS, FROM ABOUT 2 MELONS (SEE NOTE)

1 CUP FRESH LIME JUICE

1 CUP SUGAR

8 CUPS WATER

ONE 10-POUND BAG OF ICE

GARNISH: FRESH HONEYDEW OR LIME WEDGES (OPTIONAL)

Add the melon in batches to a food processor or blender and puree until smooth, stopping to scrape down the sides. Add the lime juice and sugar and process again.

Pour the melon mixture into a large serving container. Add the water and ice to the desired consistency and mix well. Serve in small cocktail glasses. Garnish, if desired.

NOTE: SUBSTITUTE WATERMELON OR CANTALOUPE.

SERVES 12–16

june bug

I love the inspiration behind this drink. Duane Richards, the bar manager at 115 Midtown in Raleigh, North Carolina, created it as a sippy-cup soother for his teething daughter. But Duane says adults love it, too—especially at a pig pickin' (pork roast) on a hot day, saying, "It's perfect for taking the heat off." One forgets how wonderful orange sherbet is until you have it in this drink, which makes *our* teeth feel pretty good, too.

25 OUNCES GINGER ALE (ABOUT 3 CUPS)

2½ OUNCES GRENADINE

2½ OUNCES FRESH ORANGE JUICE

3 SCOOPS ORANGE SHERBET

GARNISH: SMALL ORANGE WEDGES (OPTIONAL)

Combine the ginger ale, grenadine, orange juice, and sherbet in a blender, pulsing until the sherbet is well incorporated.

Pour into cocktail glasses filled with ice. Garnish, if desired.

DO TELL:

JUNE BUGS MIGHT SOUND ADORABLE, BUT REALLY, THEY'RE NOT. IT'S JUST THE NAME THAT IS. THE REAL BUG—A BEETLE THAT FEASTS ON TREES AND SHRUBS—CAN BE A REAL NUISANCE. THE TERM OF ENDEARMENT MOST LIKELY RELATES TO LITTLE CHILDREN WHO ARE BEING ADORABLY PESKY.

SERVES 4

STRAWBERRY THRILL

This beverage, essentially a virgin daiquiri, will be thick at first but will quickly melt into drinkability. Add extra orange juice if you want it more free-form. Or just do as I do and serve the drink with little spoons or straws to enjoy it both ways.

¾ CUP ROSE'S LIME JUICE

⅓ CUP SUGAR

1 CUP FRESH ORANGE JUICE

4 CUPS FROZEN WHOLE STRAWBERRIES, SLIGHTLY THAWED (SEE TIP)

GARNISH: WHOLE STRAWBERRIES (OPTIONAL)

Process the Rose's Lime Juice, sugar, and orange juice in a blender or food processor. Add half of the thawed strawberries and blend, scraping down the sides as necessary. Add remaining strawberries and blend until well incorporated. Pour into cocktail glasses. Garnish, if desired.

A TASTEFUL TIP:
SOME PEOPLE KEEP FROZEN GRAPES. ME?
FROZEN STRAWBERRIES. BEFORE FREEZING, WASH,
CUT OFF THEIR TOPS, AND SEAL IN AN AIRTIGHT
CONTAINER. LET 'EM THAW FOR AWHILE BEFORE EATING.
THOUGH THEY'RE A TAD CRESTFALLEN IN
APPEARANCE, THEY TASTE LIKE LITTLE BITES OF
STRAWBERRY SORBET.

SERVES 4

MANGO LASSI

Floral-scented mango marries beautifully with rose water here for a uniquely refreshing Indian smoothie.

3 CUPS DICED FRESH (SEE TIP; ABOUT 3 LARGE) OR FROZEN MANGO

1 CUP FRESH ORANGE JUICE

1 CUP ICE

¼ CUP HONEY

2½ TEASPOONS ROSE WATER

3 CUPS PLAIN YOGURT

GARNISH: FRESH MANGO WEDGES (OPTIONAL)

Process half of the mango, orange juice, ice, honey, rose water, and yogurt in a blender until well blended, stopping to scrape down the sides as necessary.

Pour the mixture into a serving container. Repeat process with remaining ingredients and add to the container. Mix well. Serve immediately in highball glasses. Garnish, if desired.

DO TELL:
ROSE WATER IS A STEAM-DISTILLED LIQUID FROM VERY FRAGRANT ROSES THAT ORIGINATE IN FRANCE, SPAIN, AND ITALY. IT'S MOST OFTEN USED FOR FACE CREAMS AND PERFUMES, BUT IT IS USED IN BEVERAGES AND FOOD IN THE MIDDLE AND FAR EAST.

A TASTEFUL TIP: MANGOES HAVE A LARGE, FLAT SEED AT THEIR CORE, SO YOU CAN'T JUST SLICE THROUGH ONE. THE BEST WAY AROUND THIS IS TO SLICE THE MANGO LENGTHWISE A THIRD-WAY DOWN ON EACH SIDE. SCORE EACH PORTION IN A CROSS-HATCH PATTERN, BEING CAREFUL NOT TO CUT THROUGH THE SKIN. SCRAPE OFF SECTIONED CUBES INTO A CONTAINER. REMOVE WHAT MANGO YOU CAN SURROUNDING THE SEED AND ADD TO THE CONTAINER.

SERVES 8

MINTED RASPBERRY ICED TEA

Oh, if I could only bottle and sell this; I'd make a fortune. This is pure liquid summer, smooth and minty with a gorgeous color. In Arnold Palmer fashion, it's also nice to halve this tea with lemonade, and even add some vodka. Note the baking soda here—it's to help preserve the berry color.

3 CUPS FRESH OR FROZEN RASPBERRIES, SLIGHTLY THAWED IF FROZEN

1¼ CUPS SUGAR

¼ CUP CHOPPED FRESH MINT

PINCH OF BAKING SODA

4 CUPS BOILING WATER

8 REGULAR-SIZE OR 2 FAMILY-SIZE BLACK TEA BAGS

3½ CUPS COLD WATER

GARNISH: FRESH MINT SPRIG WITH RASPBERRIES ON SMALL WOODEN SKEWERS (OPTIONAL)

Combine the raspberries and sugar in a large pitcher. Use a wooden spoon to crush the berries and mix with sugar. Add the mint and baking soda.

Add the boiling water to the tea bags in a large teapot or pan and let steep for several minutes. Discard the tea bags and let the tea concentrate cool.

Pour the tea into the raspberry mixture. Let stand for about 1 hour. Pour the raspberry-tea mixture through a strainer. Return the tea to the pitcher. Add the cold water. Cover and chill before serving in iced-tea glasses filled with ice. Garnish, if desired.

SERVES 6–8

ARNOLD PALMER

"Arnie," as my dad liked to call him as though they were good friends, stood out not only for his golfing expertise, but also for his favorite drink after hitting the greens: a nonalcoholic refresher consisting of half tea and half lemonade.

- 3 OUNCES LEMONADE
- 3 OUNCES ICED TEA, SWEET OR UNSWEETENED

GARNISH: LEMON WHEEL OR WEDGE (OPTIONAL)

Pour the lemonade and iced tea into an iced-tea glass filled with ice. Stir well. Garnish, if desired.

DO TELL:
THE CHERRY CREEK COUNTRY CLUB NEAR DENVER TAKES CREDIT FOR THIS DRINK, BUT NUMEROUS OTHER DRINKS PAYING HOMAGE TO IT HAVE POPPED UP SINCE. MY FAVORITE TWIST ON THE DRINK IS "THE TOM ARNOLD," WHICH ADDS VODKA TO THE RECIPE.

SERVES 1

CLASSIC
LEMONADE

7½ CUPS WATER

1 TO 1½ CUPS SUGAR

1 TABLESPOON LEMON ZEST
(FROM ABOUT 2 LEMONS)

1½ CUPS FRESH LEMON JUICE
(FROM ABOUT 14 LEMONS)

Boil ½ cup of the water in a medium saucepan. Add sugar to taste and the lemon zest, stirring until the sugar dissolves. Remove from the heat and stir in the lemon juice. Let cool.

Pour the lemon syrup mixture into a serving pitcher and add the remaining 7 cups water. Serve in iced tea glasses filled with ice.

MAKES 2½ QUARTS

SERVES 8

GINGER LEMONADE

Ginger adds a lovely depth of flavor to lemonade, smoothing out the tartness while at the same time adding zip, mostly to its aftertaste. A garnish of candied ginger is a nice addition to the flavor, and very thin slices of lemon nestled into the ice add even more flavorful distinction.

1 CUP GINGER SYRUP (SEE NOTE)

2½ QUARTS CLASSIC LEMONADE (PAGE 105), CHILLED

GARNISH: CANDIED GINGER ON SKEWERS, THINLY SLICED LEMON WHEELS (OPTIONAL)

Add the ginger syrup to the lemonade. Pour into ice-filled cocktail glasses. Garnish, if desired.

NOTE: FOR A HOMEMADE RECIPE, SEE PAGE 26. FOR AN ONLINE SOURCE, SEE PAGE 140.

SERVES 8–10

LUSCIOUS LIMEADE

Lemonade and porches are a given, but limeade makes for an unexpected surprise.

7½ CUPS WATER

1½ CUPS SUGAR

1 TABLESPOON LIME ZEST
(FROM ABOUT 2 LIMES)

1½ CUPS FRESH LIME JUICE
(FROM ABOUT 14 LIMES)

GARNISH: LIME WEDGES, SLICES OR
RIND CURLS (OPTIONAL)

Boil ½ cup of the water in a medium saucepan. Add the sugar and lime zest, stirring until the sugar dissolves. Remove from the heat and stir in the lime juice. Let cool.

Pour the lime syrup into a pitcher and add the remaining 7 cups water. Refrigerate until very cold. Pour into tall cocktail glasses filled with ice. Garnish, if desired.

SERVES 8

INDIAN SUMMER

What a great way to spruce up apple cider, which I didn't think was possible to make even yummier. The addition of ginger increases the rich flavor.

3½ OUNCES APPLE CIDER

1 OUNCE GINGER ALE

½ OUNCE GINGER SYRUP (SEE NOTE)

GARNISH: THIN APPLE SLICE OR CANDIED GINGER ON SKEWER (OPTIONAL)

Pour the cider, ginger ale, and ginger syrup into a cocktail glass filled with ice and stir. Garnish, if desired.

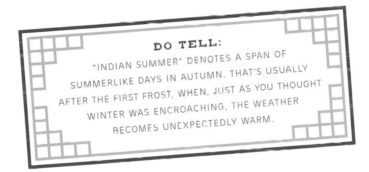

DO TELL:
"INDIAN SUMMER" DENOTES A SPAN OF SUMMERLIKE DAYS IN AUTUMN. THAT'S USUALLY AFTER THE FIRST FROST, WHEN, JUST AS YOU THOUGHT WINTER WAS ENCROACHING, THE WEATHER BECOMES UNEXPECTEDLY WARM.

NOTE: FOR A HOMEMADE RECIPE, SEE PAGE 26. FOR AN ONLINE SOURCE, SEE PAGE 140.

SERVES 1

GETTING JUICED

BEAUTIFULLY *and* SAFELY

USED TO BE, ONLY SICKENINGLY SWEET SWILL WAS AVAILABLE AS NONALCOHOLIC STAND-INS FOR CHAMPAGNE OR SPARKLING WINE. NOW, MUCH TO EVERYONE'S DELIGHT, THERE ARE INNOVATIVE CHOICES THAT ARE LIGHT AND CRISP WITH CHAMPAGNE QUALITIES.

My favorite label, SONOMA SPARKLER, originated in its namesake county in California, and its sparkling juices are made from blood oranges, peaches, pears, raspberries, Meyer lemons, and apples (at less than $5 a bottle). R. W. Knudsen also offers some distinctive sparklers in particularly nice bottles. (For sources, see page 140.)

BLUEBERRY SHRUB

This has to be one of the oldest porch drinks. My grandmother once told me it was the soft drink of her generation (that, and Coca-Cola, which, with a trace of cocaine in its early days, put a pep in her step). Shrubs make great use of fresh fruits—blueberries, blackberries, raspberries, strawberries, you name it—and are kept in concentrate form, which, tightly covered, will keep in your refrigerator for a couple of weeks (just whisk it to incorporate the sugar "foam" that forms on top). Don't be alarmed by the vinegar; the sugar and water tone it down, leaving it most enjoyable. This could be made into a punch by pouring the shrub concentrate into a large bowl and adding 12 to 14 cups of water followed by ice cubes

4 CUPS FRESH BLUEBERRIES

2 CUPS CIDER VINEGAR

2 CUPS SUGAR

GARNISH: SKEWERS OF BLUEBERRIES (OPTIONAL)

Place the blueberries in a nonmetallic container. Add the vinegar. Cover tightly and refrigerate for at least 3 days

Pour the vinegar-marinated blueberries into a sieve over a bowl, press the berries to release all their juice. Discard the solids.

Pour the blueberry liquid into a medium saucepan. Add the sugar and boil for 3 minutes, stirring occasionally. Remove from the heat and let cool. Pour the sweetened blueberry liquid into a small container and chill.

To make each drink, add ¼ cup blueberry concentrate to a medium cocktail glass filled with ice and add 1 cup cold water. Garnish, if desired.

SERVES 12–14

Nojito

This is a great twist on the *mojito*—the rustic sugarcane and rum drink of old Havana given its name in the 1930s by Sloppy Joe's bar in Key West. Here there's no rum, but the immense flavor remains. However, in this incarnation, I make it a bit differently. Not wanting a lot of little mint leaf pieces in my teeth, I've created it so that the mint flavor gets infused beforehand; I then garnish the drink with a few mint leaves for added decoration and flavor. For an alcoholic variation, see Prosecco Mojito (page 49).

12 TO 14 SMALL MINT LEAVES
(SEE NOTE)

1 OUNCE FRESH LIME JUICE

1 TABLESPOON SUPERFINE SUGAR

4 OUNCES CLUB SODA OR SELTZER WATER

GARNISH: MINT LEAVES, LIME SLICES (OPTIONAL)

Muddle the mint leaves in a cocktail shaker with the lime juice and sugar. Add ice cubes to fill a shaker and pour in the club soda. Gently shake a few times to incorporate (remember: club soda is fizzy).

Strain into a medium or tall cocktail glass filled with ice. Garnish, if desired.

NOTE: WITH LARGER MINT LEAVES, USE 6 OR 7.

SERVES 1

ROY ROGERS

This drink—a less-sweet version of a cherry cola—is as clean-cut as the legendary cowboy for whom it was named, making it a natural for little cowpokes. If you can, serve it in a festive glass, such as one in the shape of a boot (for sources, see page 140).

6 TO 8 OUNCES COCA-COLA
½ OUNCE GRENADINE

GARNISH: MARASCHINO CHERRY (OPTIONAL)

Pour the Coca-Cola and grenadine into a cocktail glass filled with ice and mix. Garnish, if desired.

DO TELL:
SOME ROY ROGERS TRIVIA: AS A LITTLE BOY, ROY TAUGHT HIMSELF HOW TO YODEL BY LISTENING TO A SWISS YODELING ALBUM OVER AND OVER AGAIN. HIS HORSE, "TRIGGER," WAS ORIGINALLY NAMED "GOLDEN CLOUD," WHICH DIDN'T HAVE THE PUNCH OF THE MONIKER ROY LATER CAME UP WITH. AFTER TRIGGER'S PASSING, ROY HAD HIM MOUNTED. THE HORSE CAN BE SEEN AT THE ROY ROGERS–DALE EVANS MUSEUM IN BRANSON, MISSOURI.

SERVES 1

SHIRLEY *temple*

Oh, how I used to love getting one of these pink little numbers so that I, too, could enjoy a "drink" with my folks. Pink as Shirley's little cheeks, it's sweet-tart in honor of the legendary curly-headed cutie.

3 OUNCES LEMON-LIME SODA

3 OUNCES GINGER ALE

1 DASH GRENADINE

GARNISH: MARASCHINO CHERRY (OPTIONAL)

Pour the lemon-lime soda and ginger ale into a cocktail glass filled with ice. Add the grenadine and stir. Garnish, if desired.

DO TELL:
THE ACTRESSES SHIRLEY JONES AND SHIRLEY MACLAINE WERE REPORTEDLY NAMED AFTER SHIRLEY TEMPLE. THE ICONIC CHILD STAR WENT ON TO BE THE UNITED STATES AMBASSADOR TO CZECHOSLOVAKIA (1989–92).

SERVES 1

SUBSTITUTE TEACHER
IN LIEU OF LIQUOR

Consider these alternatives if you're wanting beverages to be unleaded, alcohol-wise, but still packed with flavor.

APPLE LIQUEUR or APPLE BRANDY UNSWEETENED APPLE JUICE CONCENTRATE, APPLE JUICE, APPLE CIDER

BEER NONALCOHOLIC BEER, WHITE GRAPE JUICE, GINGER ALE

BOURBON NONALCOHOLIC SPARKLING WINE, SPARKLING APPLE CIDER, SPARKLING GRAPE JUICE, PEACH SYRUP, ORANGE OR PINEAPPLE JUICE, VANILLA EXTRACT

CHAMPAGNE NONALCOHOLIC SPARKLING WHITE GRAPE JUICE, LEMON-LIME SODA, SODA WATER

CHERRY LIQUEUR CHERRY SYRUP

COFFEE LIQUEUR ESPRESSO OR COFFEE SYRUP

COGNAC PEACH, PEAR, OR APRICOT NECTAR OR JUICE

ORANGE LIQUEUR UNSWEETENED ORANGE CONCENTRATE OR JUICE

PEPPERMINT SCHNAPPS MINT SYRUP (PAGE 26)

RED WINE RED GRAPE JUICE OR CRANBERRY JUICE

RUM NONALCOHOLIC RUM EXTRACT, PINEAPPLE JUICE FLAVORED WITH ALMOND EXTRACT

SAKE RICE VINEGAR

TEQUILA CACTUS JUICE OR AGAVE NECTAR

TRIPLE SEC ORANGE JUICE CONCENTRATE OR ORANGE JUICE

VODKA WHITE GRAPE JUICE MIXED WITH LIME

WHITE WINE WHITE GRAPE JUICE OR APPLE JUICE

CHAPTER

N⁰ **5**

DON'T DROWN YOUR GUESTS WITH LIQUID LOVE WITHOUT GIVING THEM SOMETHING TO KEEP THEM LEVEL-HEADED: *FOOD*. THESE SCRUMPTIOUS AND BEAUTIFUL TREATS ARE EASY TO MAKE BUT LOOK LIKE YOU TAPPED A CATERER. (AND I BET YOUR FRIENDS WILL BE PINING FOR THESE RECIPES.)

LITTLE BITES

CHEERY TOMATOES
with JALAPEÑO-PIMIENTO CHEESE

Juicy tomatoes and pimiento cheese are dreamy together. Especially when they're in bite-size form.

ABOUT 2 DOZEN LARGE CHERRY OR SMALL ROMA TOMATOES

JALAPEÑO-PIMIENTO CHEESE (RECIPE FOLLOWS)

GARNISH: JALAPEÑO SLIVERS (OPTIONAL)

Remove the stems, then cut the tomatoes in half width-wise. Use a melon baller or teaspoon to gently scoop out pulp. Place upside down on paper towels to drain.

Using a teaspoon, gently stuff Jalapeño-Pimiento Cheese into each tomato half. Garnish, if desired.

JALAPEÑO-PIMIENTO CHEESE

1 SMALL WHITE ONION, CHOPPED

3 GARLIC CLOVES

1 OR 2 JALAPEÑOS, DE-SEEDED, STEMS REMOVED, CHOPPED

½ POUND MEDIUM YELLOW CHEDDAR CHEESE, GRATED

½ POUND WHITE SHARP CHEDDAR CHEESE, GRATED

ONE 7-OUNCE JAR PIMIENTOS, DRAINED

1 CUP MAYONNAISE

WHITE PEPPER

In a food processor, finely chop the onion, garlic, and jalapeño(s).

Place the cheeses and pimientos in a medium bowl. Add the vegetables and mayonnaise and mix well. Season with white pepper.

MAKES ABOUT 4 CUPS

SERVES 8–12

greek crostini

Olives and feta—what could be better? This is insanely easy to make but leaves a sophisticated impression.

½ CUP BUTTER OR MARGARINE, AT ROOM TEMPERATURE

4 OUNCES CRUMBLED FETA CHEESE

36 SLICES FRENCH BREAD, SLICED ABOUT ½ INCH THICK AND 2½ INCHES WIDE

½ CUP CHOPPED KALAMATA OLIVES

GARNISH: FETA CHEESE AND CHOPPED OLIVES (OPTIONAL)

Preheat the oven to 400 degrees F.

Mix the butter and feta in a small bowl.

Spread about 1 teaspoon of the mixture on each slice of bread. Top with a little chopped olive. Place on a nonstick baking pan or one lightly coated with cooking spray.

Bake about 10 minutes, or until the cheese is melted and the toast edges are golden. Garnish, if desired.

DO TELL:
WHEN TIME IS SHORT, I USE PRECHOPPED MIXED OLIVES, WHICH I ADORE ON ITALIAN SANDWICHES. JUST MAKE SURE TO DRAIN THE OLIVE MIX WELL.

SERVES 12

BABY CRAB CAKES
with LEMON-GARLIC AIOLI

For a brunch or special porch party, bring out the crab. These perfectly sized bites are super-easy to eat . . . and eat.

- ¼ CUP MINCED FRESH CHIVES
- ½ CUP FINELY DICED CELERY
- ¼ CUP FINELY DICED RED BELL PEPPER
- ¼ CUP MAYONNAISE
- 1 LARGE EGG
- 1 TABLESPOON DIJON MUSTARD

- ¼ OR ½ TEASPOON HOT SAUCE
- 2 TABLESPOONS FRESH LEMON JUICE
- 1 POUND COOKED, SHELLED LUMP CRABMEAT
- 1¾ CUPS PLAIN, TOASTED BREAD CRUMBS
- LEMON-GARLIC AIOLI (FACING PAGE)
- GARNISH: CHOPPED FRESH CHIVES

Preheat the oven to 400 degrees F.

In a large bowl, combine the chives, celery, bell pepper, mayonnaise, egg, mustard, hot sauce, and lemon juice. Add the crabmeat and ¾ cup of bread crumbs. Stir very gently until just mixed.

Place the remaining 1 cup bread crumbs on a small plate. Set aside.

Using a ¼ cup measuring cup, scoop out the mix and delicately form into small round cakes (about 2 inches wide and 1 inch thick). Gently coat each cake on all sides with bread crumbs and place on lightly greased baking sheet.

Bake until golden brown, about 15 minutes. Before serving, use a squirt bottle or teaspoon to top each crab cake with the aïoli. Garnish with the fresh chives. Serve warm.

MAKES 14

SERVES 6–8

Lemon-Garlic Aioli

¼ CUP FRESH LEMON JUICE

2 TEASPOONS LEMON ZEST

1½ TEASPOONS DIJON MUSTARD

1 OR 2 TEASPOONS CHOPPED GARLIC

¼ CUP MAYONNAISE

HOT SAUCE

½ CUP OLIVE OIL

FRESHLY GROUND BLACK PEPPER

SEA SALT

Place the lemon juice, lemon zest, mustard, garlic, mayonnaise, and a couple dashes of hot sauce into the work bowl of a food processor and blend until smooth.

With the machine running, slowly add the olive oil until incorporated, scraping down the sides as necessary. Season with pepper, salt, and more hot sauce.

MAKES ABOUT 1 CUP

A
TASTEFUL

WHILE YOU'RE MAKING THIS SAUCE, DOUBLE THE RECIPE AND STORE IT IN A CAPPED SQUIRT BOTTLE (WHICH MAKES TOPPING EACH CRAB CAKE A BREEZE). THE AIOLI IS DELICIOUS WITH FISH, STEAK, OR FRENCH FRIES, AND KEEPS WELL IN THE REFRIGERATOR FOR ABOUT TWO WEEKS.

TIP

NOTE: IF CRAB CAKES DON'T GET BROWN ENOUGH, BROIL ABOUT A MINUTE BEFORE SERVING OR TURN HALFWAY THROUGH COOKING.

easy eats:
NIBBLES IN A PINCH

*WHEN TIME IS SHORT BUT EXPECTATIONS ARE HIGH,
TURN TO THESE QUICK APPETIZERS.*

ANTIPASTO PLATTER featuring a mix of artichoke hearts, roasted red and yellow bell peppers, grilled veggies from the deli, pickled banana peppers, small slices of artisan bread, sliced Genoa salami, olives, dried figs, and slices of fresh mozzarella

CASHEWS, roasted or seasoned

CHEESE TORTELLINI cooked al dente, marinated for a few hours in just enough Italian dressing to lightly coat

BLOCK OR SMALL MOLD OF CREAM CHEESE topped with chutney or hot pepper jelly

CUCUMBER SLICES topped with herbed cream cheese

CHIPS, distinctively flavored or rustically made

EDAMAME cooked in boiling salted water for 8 to 10 minutes; drained and sprinkled with ground sea salt

GUACAMOLE, salsas, and tortilla chips

HUMMUS and toasted pita chips

VARIETY OF OLIVES (remember to have small dishes for the pits)

PROSCIUTTO-WRAPPED MELON SLICES

POPCORN, plain or flavored, served in vintage-style popcorn bags or small Chinese-takeout containers (for sources, see page 140)

ROASTED PEANUTS, husks on

THIN SLICES OF SAUSAGE AND GOOD CHEESE with bread or crackers

COOL-AS-A-CUCUMBER
SMOKED SALMON SANDWICHES

These sandwiches are perfect as a cooling snack. They're served open-faced because the filling's too lovely to hide.

LEMON-DILL SAUCE (FACING PAGE), CHILLED FOR AT LEAST 30 MINUTES

24 SLICES GOOD-QUALITY COCKTAIL BREAD

24 THIN SLICES (ABOUT 8 OUNCES) SMOKED SALMON

24 THIN-CUT SLICES ENGLISH CUCUMBER

GARNISH: 24 SMALL SPRIGS BABY DILL

Spread ½ heaping teaspoon of the Lemon-Dill Sauce onto each slice of bread, focusing on the center of the slice and avoiding the far edges (to avoid a messy look). Press an appropriately sized slice of smoked salmon into the sauce. Top each with a slice of cucumber. Garnish with a small dill sprig.

Serve right away, or cover lightly in a sealed container or on a plastic wrap–covered plate or platter, and refrigerate for a few hours in advance.

A TASTEFUL TIP:
USE WIDE, THIN-SLICED SCOTTISH-STYLE SALMON
IF POSSIBLE, SINCE OTHER VERSIONS CAN APPEAR
A BIT SHREDDED. ALSO, TRY OUT VARIOUS
COCKTAIL BREADS AT YOUR GOURMET DELI.
SUBSTITUTE LIGHTLY TOASTED BAGUETTE SLICES
OR PITA WEDGES IF DESIRED. ALSO, BABY DILL
IS SMALLER AND WISPIER THAN MORE MATURE
DILL, BUT EITHER WILL DO.

MAKES 24

SERVES 6–8

LEMON-DILL SAUCE

I always double this recipe to have extra sauce for cooking fish or meat later on.

⅓ CUP SOUR CREAM

⅓ CUP MAYONNAISE

1 SMALL SHALLOT, FINELY CHOPPED

2 TEASPOONS CHOPPED FRESH DILL

1 TEASPOON LEMON ZEST

1½ TEASPOONS FRESH LEMON JUICE

Combine all of the ingredients in a small bowl and mix well. Refrigerate at least 30 minutes before using.

MAKES ABOUT ⅔ CUP

SHRIMP and TOMATO
SALAD

The marriage of sweet tomatoes and shrimp, with a kiss of light and lemony cream sauce, makes for both a well-seasoned and well-dressed nibble. Serve it in small decorative bowls, avocado halves, or martini glasses.

1½ POUNDS COOKED, PEELED, AND DEVEINED LARGE (26- TO 30-COUNT) SHRIMP

1½ POUNDS GRAPE OR SMALL CHERRY TOMATOES, HALVED

¼ CUP CHOPPED SCALLIONS

2 TABLESPOONS CHOPPED FRESH BASIL OR DILL

1 TEASPOON LEMON ZEST

¼ CUP FRESH LEMON JUICE

¼ CUP SOUR CREAM OR MAYONNAISE (SEE NOTE)

1 TABLESPOON DIJON MUSTARD

SALT

WHITE PEPPER

GARNISH: LEMON ZEST, LEMON WEDGES, OR GREEN ONIONS (OPTIONAL)

Place the shrimp, tomatoes, green onions, basil, and lemon zest in a large bowl. Set aside.

Stir together the lemon juice, sour cream, and mustard in a small bowl. Gently fold into the shrimp-tomato mixture. Season with salt and pepper.

Refrigerate at least 6 to 8 hours before serving. Garnish, if desired.

NOTE: SOUR CREAM WILL LEND A LIGHTER TEXTURE, REVEALING MORE OF A LEMON AND HERB FLAVOR; MAYONNAISE WILL GIVE A CREAMIER CONSISTENCY.

SERVES 6–8

RED-DEVILED EGGS
with CRISPY BACON CRUMBLES

The name of this recipe was inspired by the deviled eggs' use of paprika, bacon, and hot sauce, which gives the filling a rusty hue and smoky flavor.

12 HARD-BOILED EGGS

6 SLICES THICK-CUT BACON, COOKED UNTIL CRISP; FINELY CRUMBLED

2 TEASPOONS SMOKED PAPRIKA

3 TABLESPOONS YELLOW MUSTARD

2 TABLESPOONS SPICY OR REGULAR PICKLE RELISH

2 TO 3 TABLESPOONS GRATED ONION

2 TABLESPOONS MAYONNAISE

HOT SAUCE

SEA SALT

BLACK PEPPER, FRESHLY GROUND

GARNISH: PAPRIKA, CRUMBLED BACON (OPTIONAL)

Peel the eggs under cool running water. Slice the eggs in half lengthwise, gently scooping out the cooked yolk into a medium bowl. Add the bacon, paprika, mustard, relish, onion, and mayonnaise. Stir well and season with hot sauce, salt, and pepper.

Using a spoon (or for fancier looking eggs, an icing piping bag), add the filling carefully to the egg-white halves and place into a serving container. Refrigerate at least an hour before serving. Garnish, if desired.

MAKES 24

FIG *and* WALNUT
BRIE

Sun-dried fig spread is a perfect partner with cheese, and it offers exceptional Mediterranean flair. In looks, think of this as a large Brie-fig sandwich. Pear and apple slices make nice accompaniments.

ONE 16-OUNCE WHEEL BRIE CHEESE

ONE 8.5-OUNCE JAR DALMATIA FIG SPREAD (SEE SOURCES, PAGE 140)

1 CUP CHOPPED WALNUTS

BAGUETTE OR PITA BREAD SLICES, OR CRACKERS

Trim the rind from the top of the Brie, leaving ½ inch of rind around the edges.

Slice the Brie in half horizontally. Spoon half of the fig spread over the bottom half of the Brie. Sprinkle with half of the walnuts. Cover the top half of the Brie. Cover tightly with plastic wrap and refrigerate for several hours or overnight.

Preheat the oven to 350 degrees F.

Remove the plastic wrap and place the cheese in a small baking dish. Top the Brie round with the remaining fruit spread and walnuts, focusing on the center.

Bake 12 to 15 minutes or until the cheese is melted. Serve immediately with baguette or pita bread slices, or assorted crackers.

SERVES 12–14

ASPARAGUS-PROSCIUTTO PUFFS

These filling little numbers are both lovely and easy to make.

24 SMALL TO MEDIUM (NOT THIN)
ASPARAGUS SPEARS

ONE 17.3-OUNCE PACKAGE FROZEN
PUFF PASTRY, THAWED

ONE 5.2-OUNCE PACKAGE BOURSIN
OR HERBED CREAM CHEESE

12 SLICES OF PROSCIUTTO, HALVED

Preheat the oven to 400 degrees F.

Trim the asparagus to 5 to 6 inches in length

Place the asparagus in a pot of boiling water until crisp-tender, about 3 minutes. Remove from the water with slotted spoon and drain.

Spread out both puff pastry portions and slice both in half vertically, making four sections. Slice each section horizontally into six equal-size strips about 3 inches wide by 2 inches long.

Spread ½ teaspoon of the cream cheese onto each pastry strip, avoiding the edges, and top with a prosciutto slice, folded to fit atop the cheese. Add one asparagus spear at the top of the prosciutto and cheese and roll into a slim bundle, pinching the dough together to firmly seal.

Place the pastry bundles seam-side down on a nonstick baking sheet lined with parchment paper. (Do not use a greased baking sheet or the bundle will be soggy.) Bake until the bundles are puffed and golden, about 10 minutes. Place on wire racks to cool slightly before serving.

MAKES 24

CREAMY ORANGE FRUIT DIP

We lean too heavily on savory dips for parties, so why not have a sweet one? This is like a dippable whipped orange cheesecake. Serve it with firmer fruits—apples, pears, nectarines, strawberries, and the like. Use leftover dip to top brownies or spread on coffee cake.

ONE 8-OUNCE PACKAGE CREAM CHEESE, SOFTENED

2 CUPS POWDERED SUGAR

2 TEASPOONS VANILLA EXTRACT

½ CUP ORANGE MARMALADE

1 CUP WHIPPED CREAM

ASSORTED FRUITS

GARNISH: THIN ORANGE PEEL STRIPS (OPTIONAL)

In a large bowl, combine the cream cheese, powdered sugar, and vanilla with an electric mixer at medium speed. Add the marmalade and whipped cream and combine gently until blended. Refrigerate until chilled. Serve with assorted fruits. Garnish, if desired.

MAKES ABOUT 3 CUPS

KEEP YOUR COOL (& YOUR HEAT)
FOOD SAFETY

When entertaining outside during warm weather, IT'S EASY TO FORGET THAT FOOD CAN BECOME DANGEROUS TO EAT IF NOT KEPT AT THE PROPER TEMPERATURE. WHAT'S MORE, BEING OUTDOORS (ESPECIALLY AROUND DRINKING HOSTS) OFTEN LEADS TO TOSSING FOOD SAFETY CONCERNS TO THE FOUR WINDS. THAT'S NEVER GOOD. CONSIDER THESE POINTERS.

KEEP ICE AND PERISHABLES IN SEPARATE CHESTS to avoid having the perishables subjected to warm air due to the constant opening of the chest's lid. In the perishables cooler, use a thermometer to be sure the temperature stays at or below 40 degrees F.

KEEP A SCOOP ON THE OUTSIDE OF THE ICE CONTAINER so as not to introduce bacteria into the ice.

FORGET THE NOTION OF A "SEASONED" GRILL—it's simply just a dirty grill. Before firing it up, make sure it's clean by scrubbing it with hot, soapy water.

USE A MEAT THERMOMETER to make sure meats are cooked to their proper temperature:

ALL POULTRY: 165 DEGREES F

HAMBURGERS (BEEF): 160 DEGREES F

ALL CUTS OF PORK: 160 DEGREES F

BEEF, VEAL, AND LAMB
(STEAKS, ROASTS, AND CHOPS):
MEDIUM-RARE 145 DEGREES F
MEDIUM 160 DEGREES F

NEVER BASTE COOKED MEAT WITH ITS MARINADE (which contains bacteria from the raw meat); if you insist you need it, bring it to a boil before using. Better yet, always make more marinade than you need (reserving some for final flavoring) so you won't have such an issue.

NEVER PUT COOKED MEAT on the same bacteria-laden platter that once held raw meat.

KEEPING FOOD ON ICE IS A MUST IF IT'S MEANT TO STAY COOL. According to the United States Department of Agriculture's Food Safety and Inspection Service, there is no such thing as a "two-hour rule" when it comes to leaving food out on a table. In 90-degree weather, the most you can feel good about is one hour—after that, off to the refrigerator it goes. If food is meant to stay hot, keep it in a slow cooker or chafing dish at 140 degrees F or warmer. A good thermometer will help you know where the food stands.

SPEAKING OF WHERE THE FOOD STANDS, keep it out of direct sunlight, which intensifies its temperature.

REFRIGERATE LEFTOVERS PROMPTLY. Discard any food left out for 2 hours or more.

SOURCES

⫸⟶ *Agua fresca* jars Mexican grocers or *MexGrocer.com* (for plastic ones) or *eBay.com* (glass ones in two sizes) ⫸⟶ Boot glass *eBay.com* or various online retailers ⫸⟶ Chimayo chile powder gourmet grocers or *MadeInNewMexico.com* ⫸⟶ Takeout cartons *MrTakeOutBags.com* or *Beau-Coup.com* ⫸⟶ Coco Lopez Cream of Coconut (15-ounce can: *CocoLopez.com*) or Coco Real Cream of Coconut (21-ounce squeeze bottle); Liquor stores or *Liquorama.net* ⫸⟶ Dalmatia Fig Spread gourmet grocers or *DalmatiaImports.com* ⫸⟶ Dried hibiscus flowers/pods (*jamaica* in Spanish): Mexican and Caribbean grocers or *MexGrocer.com* ⫸⟶ Ginger syrup (Monin): gourmet grocers, *LollicupStore.com*, or *EverythingCoffee-Tea.com*

⫸⟶ Green tea liqueur (Zen Green Tea Liqueur): liquor stores or *BevMo.com* ⫸⟶ Novelty ice trays Ikea and Target stores ⫸⟶ R.W. Knudsen sparkling beverages gourmet grocers or *KnudsenJuice.com*, *ShopNaturalHealth.net*, *OrganicMall.com*, *MannaHarvest.net*, and *WellnessGrocer.com* ⫸⟶ Santa Cruz Organic Juices gourmet grocers or *SCoJuice.com* ⫸⟶ Sonoma Sparkler gourmet grocers or *SonomaCider.com* or *Amazon.com* ⫸⟶ Vintage-style popcorn bags/tubs *Tias.com*, *HT-Accessories.com*, *Concession-Supply.com*, or *MaharDryGoods.com* ⫸⟶ Wooden skewers, small Gourmet food retailers or *Amazon.com*. *AceMart.com*, or *WebstaurantStore.com*.

PERMISSIONS

⫸⟶ Gumby Slumber recipe (page 50) used with permission of Little Palm Island Resort & Spa ⫸⟶ Pitcher of Juleps recipe (page 68) used with permission from its creator, Stanley Dry ⫸⟶ Image of Hotel Del Coronado porch balcony used with permission of the Hotel Del Coronado ⫸⟶ Strawberry Martini recipe (page 39) used with permission of Sushi Samba, Dallas ⫸⟶ June Bug recipe (page 97) used with permission of Midtown & Bar 115 in Raleigh, North Carolina.

INDEX

TABLE OF EQUIVALENTS

LIQUID / DRY MEASURES

U.S.	METRIC
DASH / 1/8 OUNCE	2 MILLILITERS
BAR SPOON / 1/2 OUNCE	15 MILLILITERS
1/4 TEASPOON	1.25 MILLILITERS
1/2 TEASPOON	2.5 MILLILITERS
1 TEASPOON	5 MILLILITERS
1 TABLESPOON (3 TEASPOONS)	15 MILLILITERS
2 TABLESPOONS (PONY) 1 FLUID OUNCE	30 MILLILITERS
3 TABLESPOONS (JIGGER) 1 1/2 FLUID OUNCES	45 MILLILITERS
1/4 CUP	60 MILLILITERS
1/3 CUP	80 MILLILITERS
1/2 CUP	120 MILLILITERS
2/3 CUP	160 MILLILITERS
3/4 CUP	180 MILLILITERS
1 CUP	240 MILLILITERS
1 PINT (2 CUPS)	480 MILLILITERS
1 QUART (4 CUPS or 32 OUNCES)	960 MILLILITERS
1 GALLON (4 QUARTS)	3.84 LITERS

1 MEDIUM LEMON....3 TABLESPOONS JUICE
1 MEDIUM LIME..1 1/2–2 TABLESPOONS JUICE
1 MEDIUM ORANGE....1/3 CUP JUICE

LENGTH

U.S.	METRIC
1/8 INCH	3 MILLIMETERS
1/4 INCH	6 MILLIMETERS
1/2 INCH	12 MILLIMETERS
1 INCH	2.5 CENTIMETERS

OVEN TEMPERATURE

FAHRENHEIT	CELSIUS	GAS
250	120	1/2
275	140	1
300	150	2
325	160	3
350	180	4
375	190	5
400	200	6
425	220	7
450	230	8
475	240	9
500	260	10